560

D0557676

1

Celibacy, Prayer and Friendship

Celibacy, Prayer and Friendship

A MAKING-SENSE-OUT-OF-LIFE APPROACH

CHRISTOPHER KIESLING, O. P.

ALBA · HOUSE   NEW · YORK

SOCIETY OF ST. PAUL, 2187 VICTORY BLVD., STATEN ISLAND, NEW YORK 10314

Library of Congress Cataloging in Publication Data

Kiesling, Christopher.
    Celibacy, prayer, and friendship.

    1. Celibacy. 2. Monastic and religious life.
3. Prayer. 4. Friendship. I. Title.
BV4390.K48   253'.2   77-25084
ISBN 0-8189-0365-1

Nihil Obstat:
Raymond T. Powers, S.T.D.
Censor Librorum

Imprimatur:
✠*James P. Mahoney, D.D.*
Vicar General, Archdiocese of New York
December 10, 1977

*The Nihil Obstat and Imprimatur
are a declaration that a book or pamphlet is considered
to be free from doctrinal or moral error. It is not implied
that those who have granted the Nihil Obstat and
Imprimatur agree with the contents,
opinions or statements expressed.*

*Produced in the United States of
America by the Fathers and Brothers of the
Society of St. Paul, 2187 Victory Boulevard,
Staten Island, New York, 10314, as part of their
communications apostolate.*

5 6 7 8 9 (Current Printing: first digit).

TO FRIENDS

Acknowledgments

I wish to thank the editor of **Review for Religious** for permission to use in the course of this book material in revised form from an article entitled "Celibacy, Friendship, and Prayer," which appeared in that journal, volume 30 (1970), pages 595-617. I likewise thank the editor of **Cross and Crown** for permission to use the material in this book's fourth chapter. which appeared in that journal, volume 27 (1975). pages 239-254. under the title "Celibacy: An Adventure in Living." All translations of the Scriptures are from the New American Bible and are used with permission of the copyright holder, The Confraternity of Christian Doctrine. Washington, D. C.

No small debt of gratitude is owed to Ursula Klocke, who typed much of the first draft of this book, and to Loretta Crippes, who finished the typing of the first draft and did the whole of the final draft. Benedict Ashley, O.P.. and Joanne Lucid, B.V.M.. did me the favor of reading the manuscript and offering suggestions for its improvement. I thank them for the care with which they read the work and for the ideas they proposed. I assume responsibility, however, for the final product.

Lastly, I owe thanks to many people who showed interest and encouragement in the course of the three years in which I struggled to complete this book in the midst of other duties.

Christopher Kiesling, O.P.

CONTENTS

Introduction

This book presents a personal view of celibacy, prayer, and friendship. An effort to describe celibacy from the inside, it is the result of reflection on personal experience. It is not the product of methodical scholarly research but of years of making sense out of my own life and helping others to make sense out of theirs.

The value of this approach to celibacy was impressed upon me in the summer of 1968. In that year the United Methodist pastors of Montana were aware of the renewal that was going on in the Roman Catholic Church. To familiarize themselves more thoroughly with the renewal, they decided to have an entire Roman Catholic faculty for their annual week-long summer school. I was one of the three priests invited to serve.

The circumstances of the summer school were idyllic. The location was high in the mountains of Montana at Luccock Campgrounds, near Livingston. The pastors came with their wives and children. They occupied a number of cabins on the campgrounds or lived in campers, trailers, or tents. The mornings were devoted to lectures and discussions of particular themes, the evenings to wide-range dialogue with the three priests. Programs were provided for the children in such a way that most of the wives were free to attend the morning lectures and evening discussions. The afternoons were free for enjoying mountain hikes, ball games, swimming, or just lazily watching a clear mountain stream tumble over rocks and logs on its way down to sea level. Worship together, conversation over delicious meals, song fests, and late night discussions enriched the days. The spirit of community and friendliness among these people was remarkable. An appropriate symbol of their spirit was the ease and gusto with which they would break into song at unexpected moments.

On the opening Monday evening, we assembled in the large building which served as lecture hall and dining room. After I gave a short talk introducing the theme for the week, we three priests answered the pastors' questions about a variety of topics, getting acquainted with each other. A few days before, Pope Paul VI had issued **Humanae Vitae.** Its contents had been reported in all the newspapers. Naturally the exchange eventually reached the Roman Catholic Church's position on birth control. That topic led to the Church's teaching on marriage, divorce, sex, and related matters, among them celibacy. The usual questions were asked about celibacy and we priests responded with the standard answers.

In the course of this discussion I sensed that we were failing to convey to our audience what celibacy really is. We were not helping them to see the celibate experience from the inside, so to speak. We were explaining the different rationales behind the celibacy of the diocesan priest and the celibacy of the man or woman in a religious community. We were stating familiar motives for celibacy: following the example of Christ, giving undivided attention to God, freedom for ministry, bearing witness to the transcendence of the kingdom of God, and so on. But we were not showing how these motives operated in the lives of celibates. We were not revealing the aspirations, the struggles, the doubts, the convictions, the fears, the loves, the joys which make up the life of celibates. I left the evening discussion feeling frustrated.

As the next couple of days unfolded, I fell in love with these people, so good, warm, and friendly were they. I felt at home with them and free among them. But I was haunted by that very shallow discussion of celibacy the first night. I gradually made a decision. On the final morning of the week, each of the three priests was to make a final presentation. Although the field for which I had been engaged was renewal in worship, I decided that I would talk about celibacy. I would try to share with these people my personal experience of celibacy. These people had won my heart and I felt that I could lay it open to them.

When we assembled the final morning, I began by recounting my reaction to the first evening's discussion of celibacy and the decision I had reached during the week. I confessed that I was frightened by what I was going to do: share with the whole assembly what I had never shared even with individuals. I likened it to one of them standing before the group and telling everyone what it was like to love his wife or her husband. People seldom make public speeches about that subject. I then proceeded to recall my memories about my choice of celibacy, to indicate the values I had found in it, and to describe the human affection I had experienced with my fellow religious, with other men and women, and with one religious sister in particular. As I progressed I became more confident, more eloquent, and more free emotionally. By the time I finished I had tears in my eyes. So did most of the people in the room.

When I had concluded, I walked from the lectern and sat on one of the benches among the people. Silence filled the room. Then suddenly one of the women leapt up and sang out: "Glory to God, glory! O Praise the name of the Lord!" The whole assembly rose to their feet and heartily sang the doxology several times. One of the pastors approached me from behind, laid his hand on my shoulder, bent over, and said softly in my ear: "The world is a better place because of you."

Similar though less dramatic occurrences since 1968 have led me to the conviction that the most helpful "explanations" of religiously motivated celibacy are those which deal with it in terms of personal experience. Much of human life issues from sexual instinct and the need for affection; all of life is conditioned to some degree by these factors. How to envision and manage these very intimate, deep, and pervasive feelings is what prospective and actual celibates are eager to learn. How celibates understand and handle these feelings is what baffles non-celibates. The most helpful way to answer these questions—or, rather, to enable people to answer them for themselves—is by the testimony of celibates to their own experiences of celibacy. Of minimal practical help to anyone are discourses on celibacy which is nobody's celibacy.

Though flowing out of my personal experience, this book is not in the form of a story. My personal experience fits into, and has been shaped by, the historical religious community—Roman Catholic Church—and the national culture in which I have been reared and have lived. Therefore my experience has been inter-action with the understandings and values set forth in Church and society. These understandings and values have formed me and I in turn have interpreted them, judged them, and assigned them places in my personal vision and value system. This book is an expression of my understanding and evaluation of celibacy, prayer, and friendship.

That understanding and evaluation take into account Christian doctrine, Roman Catholic Church teaching, and theology, as well as philosophical, literary, and scientific insights on these subjects. Various authors, therefore, are referred to throughout the book. They are not cited, however, because they remain the only ones worth being mentioned after extensive research. The authors cited find their way into this book because they have provided me in the course of my life with ideas or value judgments which have helped me to put together a personal view and appreciation of celibacy, prayer, and friendship.

In 1971 I published an article in **Review for Religious** with a title similar to that of this book — "Celibacy, Friendship, and Prayer." (Why I switched "Friendship" and "Prayer" in the title of the book will become apparent in chapters five and nine.) The response I received from that article far exceeds the response I have had from any other publication. Besides numerous oral comments, I have received letters from all over the world—from eight of the United States, from England and Belgium, from Guatemala, Brazil, and the West Indies, from Israel, from New Guinea, New Zealand, and Australia. Even today an occasional letter arrives from someone who stumbled over the article while paging through back volumes of **Review for Religious** in some library or while sifting through a stack of old magazines sent to the foreign missions.

Many letters have simply been words of appreciation. Other letters raised questions about what was said in the article. Some have sought advice. These last have saddened me. What a shame that people cannot find in their own communities or localities understanding brothers and sisters in whom they could confide, but instead they have to write half way around the world for help!

The article, obviously helpful to many, is now entombed among back issues of magazines on remote shelves in libraries. I have given thought to questions which were raised about the article when it was published. Since it appeared, I have experienced several more years of celibate life, prayer, and friendship and have counseled more people. For these reasons I decided to expand the article into this book.

The genesis of the book suggests its limitations. Obviously, it does not say everything that could be said about celibacy, prayer, and friendship. It does not even say everything that **should** be said. The book answers questions which I have had over the course of my life. Other people may not have those questions but different ones. In regard to questions which others share with me, my answers and theirs may not correspond. What is said about prayer reflects where I am in the development of my spiritual life. It is not offered as the norm for everyone's prayer but as an example of how one person sees and practices prayer in relationship to celibacy and friendship. The chapters on human friendship have been shaped not only by the histories of my interpersonal relationships but also by questions put to me as a result of the article in **Review for Religious**. Limitations flow also from the facts that the author is male and that his celibacy, prayer, and friendships occur in the context of religious life and community. Women and diocesan priests may have other views and values than are expressed here.

By the approach I have adopted, I hope to convey some idea of what celibacy is like "from the inside," as I have phrased it previously in this introduction. Perhaps other people, even those to whom celibacy is unacceptable, will be able to identify with the feelings, struggles, questions, doubts, sacrifices, and satisfactions to which I refer and thus see into celibacy beyond ecclesiastical legislation about it and beyond the negative understanding of it as not being married.

My chief aim, however, is to stimulate religious celibates and prospective celibates each to look into her or his own life in order to bring together understanding and practice of celibacy, prayer, and friendship. Celibacy without prayer can lead only to an aching void in life. Prayer without friendship risks failing to love God authentically for want of love of neighbor. Friendship without prayer misses that important essence which makes celibacy livable and worth venturing upon—profound union with God.

The meaning of some words must be clarified before we move into our presentation. **Celibacy** does not mean simply "living alone." Many celibates do not live alone but in communities. Nor does **celibacy** mean simply "unmarried." The celibates we are talking about in this book not only are unmarried but also endeavor to forego all directly willful indulgence in the pleasures of genital sex, whether with others or alone. Being unmarried, moreover, is only a negative aspect of celibacy which, from another point of view, flows from the choice of a positive goal towards which one strives. Nor is celibacy the same as being single, in contrast to being married. A single person, in the parlance of Roman Catholic theology, is an unmarried person who is open to marriage. The proverbial old bachelor and spinster are people who never found the right partners, or who had to let them pass by because circumstances prevented marriage. The celibate, on the other hand, is unmarried and intends to remain so. This intention, moreover, is usually expressed in a promise or vow to God to be absolutely chaste.

More will be said in the course of this book about all these matters so summarily stated here, but it is necessary to understand from the beginning that in speaking about celibacy we are referring to a positive way of life which has definite characteristics and a religious quality determined by a long history within the Christian tradition. We are not referring to a merely incidental situation of not being married.

In the paragraph before the last, we referred to "genital sex." It is important to keep in mind that sex is not limited to the distinctive reproductive bodily organs of men and women and to the physical activities and particular sensual pleasures which are involved in the use of those organs. Besides physical, or genital sex, there is psychological sex. Men and women complement, respond to, and find pleasure in, one another at other levels of their persons than their bodies. Sexual attraction, interaction, and enjoyment are psychological—at the levels of mind, will, emotion, feeling—as well as physical. When the words **sex, sexual, sexuality** occur in these pages, therefore, the reader will wish to note the context and not be too quick to interpret them as referring to certain bodily activities or gratifications.

Love and **friendship** are two slippery words because of their multiple meanings. We will define them as we go along. Each bears more than one legitimate meaning, however, so the context in which each is used must be considered to ascertain which meaning it is bearing at a particular time. In regard to the word love, the principal forewarning is not to interpret it too readily as referring to physical love-making or the desire for it when the context is man and woman. Other forms of love are possible between man and woman. The word friendship is used in a broad, comprehensive sense throughout the book, but in certain places it is given a very specific meaning.

We begin this personal view by trying to answer the question why anyone chooses celibacy. The attempt to answer that question will lead us to see the mysterious quality of a vocation to celibate life. In the second chapter we will notice how conscious motives for choosing celibacy vary from person to person and in the course of the same person's life. Celibate life is not a mold reducing every celibate to the same shape, nor is an individual's celibacy marked by drab sameness from beginning to end. Chapter three develops further the dynamic quality of celibacy and its interpersonal character. A pledge of celibacy is not an end to life but the beginning of an adventure in living, as chapter four will describe it.

Essentially celibacy is an adventure in friendship with God and with other men and women. The friendship with the triune God, expressed in prayer, is the subject of chapters five and six. Chapter seven begins consideration of friendship with fellow human beings. That chapter simply calls attention to the many kinds of affection which are found in celibate life. That life is far from an arid desert void of feelings of belonging, tenderness, and warmth. Chapter eight begins a focus on highly emotional friendship in celibate life, taking love between man and woman as an example of that sort of relationship. How such friendship fits into celibate life and is related to prayer are topics of chapter eight. Chapter nine takes up different responses which people have toward the theme of chapter eight. The difficulties of celibate love noted in chapter ten lead to an examination of the relationship between celibacy and poverty in the final chapter.

Celibacy, Prayer and Friendship

Chapter 1

A MYSTERIOUS CALL

Why live celibately? Attempts to answer that question are rarely satisfactory. After they are over, I seldom feel any more certain about the value of celibacy for myself or for others. The traditional reasons brought forward do not seem compelling. Some of them are generalities which do not move me and are open to so many exceptions in terms of real life and real people that they appear useless. Some are neutralized by persuasive counter-arguments. Those who have chosen marriage are not moved to change their minds by the reasons offered for celibacy. The resolve of those who have chosen celibacy is not seriously shaken by the apparent weakness of the traditional reasons or by forceful conclusions in opposition. If I had not finally decided one way or the other about celibate life, I would leave these discussions perplexed and wondering how I would ever arrive at a sure decision.

The question deserves an answer. It challenges young people contemplating religious life or the commitment to celibacy associated with the transitional diaconate and the priesthood, sometimes also with the permanent diaconate. The question haunts some celibates most of their lives. They are not half-hearted in their religious dedication or unsure of their vocation and weighing another choice. They simply wonder occasionally why they have chosen and continue to choose a style of life which foregoes experiences which most men and women consider impossible to do without and which never cease to be attractive. The question poignantly presents itself to celibates from time to time when they meet married people who appear to have combined the appealing human fulfillment of marriage with zeal and service for God's kingdom—the very zeal and service for which the celibates renounced the attractions and satisfactions of marriage! If religious celibates experience love between man and woman, the question becomes especially pressing.

Why are efforts to discover convincing and moving reasons for celibacy so often unsatisfactory? Are the reasons for celibacy inadequate? Does the difficulty of justifying celibacy imply something worth noting about that way of life? Indeed, why all the pains to offer reasons for celibacy when scarcely anyone is making a comparable effort on behalf of marriage?

Let us take up the last question first. Why all the apologies for celibacy? Why do people ask celibates why they chose that style of life, while no one asks married people why they chose marriage? One may answer that reasons must be given for celibacy because it is not natural, whereas marriage is. But this answer presents problems.

If **marriage** means "getting married," we may agree that marriage is natural in the sense that most people spontaneously find it appealing and follow their attraction. But if marriage refers to a happy and enriching lifelong bond between a man and a woman, we may rightly wonder how natural marriage is when one out of four marriages ends in divorce and another two of the four are unhappy. Marriage as a way of life appears to be no more natural than celibacy. Both have to be worked at; both call for an art of living and for a discipline of

nature's instincts and personal inclinations of temperament and character.

The word **natural** is ambiguous. It may simply mean
following impulses. But if natural excludes control of
instincts, then human nature does not designate anything superior to animal nature. Control and discipline,
however, are natural to human beings as intelligent and
free; otherwise all the arts are unnatural. In this perspective, the celibate way of life is as natural as the married
way, though the discipline it calls for is different.

Considering celibacy as unnatural may be a cultural
phenomenon. Our society by and large provides no place
for the single person, the divorced, and the widowed.
The institutions and customs of our society are geared
to couples, presumably married and probably with children. Adults who are not married suffer in our society.
Religious celibates suffer too, though perhaps not as
much, for they have chosen their unmarried status and
its social consequences. But society's tendency to reject
any other way of life than the married does not mean
that the others are unnatural. An individual may be more
comfortable living a celibate life than a married life.
People marry because they feel more comfortable living
in marriage than outside of it or they marry one person
rather than another because they feel more comfortable
with that one. Yet no one claims they are acting un-
naturally.

To suggest that someone may be a religious celibate
because he or she feels satisfied living celibately may be
offensive to pious ears. Is not religious celibacy for the
sake of God's kingdom? If someone chooses religious
celibacy because he or she feels like living that life, is
that truly religious celibacy?

Celibacy for the sake of the kingdom does not mean
that celibacy must necessarily be a disagreeable way
of living and its choice always painful violence against

one's self. It means that celibacy, whether assumed easily or with a struggle, is directed to the kingdom of God.

Religious celibacy may be a generally acceptable, comfortable, and gratifying style of life for some people. They need not be defensive about it, any more than married people are defensive about marriage. Still, celibate life involves some struggle. If celibacy is not unnatural, it is unusual. By choice celibates forego the usual way of developing their human potential and meeting human needs, and therefore they encounter difficulties entailing varying degrees of struggle, depending on the personalities involved. Nevertheless, even struggling celibates do not find celibacy totally disagreeable; if they did, they could not, and today do not, endure it. From some point of view they find it sufficiently good to continue living it. We may conclude that **the** reason why a particular person chooses religious celibacy is that he or she feels comfortable in that way of life, even though it may entail hardship.

Two objections may be raised to this conclusion. The first is that some celibates are discontented in their celibacy yet remain celibate. The exodus from religious life and the priesthood after Vatican Council II has made us aware of how much suffering some celibates have been enduring. Religious celibates venturing into the so-called third way also witness to uncomfortableness with celibacy.

In answer it may be said that some religious celibates may be dissatisfied with celibacy's presumed requirements in respect to the relations between the sexes, and yet these celibates remain in celibate life because other aspects of that way of life are gratifying. For example, they may enjoy a certain independence which celibacy affords, or they may accept it as a condition required for the pastoral work which they greatly love. Be that as it may, people's leaving religious life and the priesthood, and the widespread acceptance of these departures, indicate public recognition of the fact that celibates should find that way of life basically satisfying or get out of it. Some religious and priests who have left have acknowledged that they did not feel sufficiently at ease with celibacy and therefore did not belong in that way of life. Whether they should have felt that way is another question, to which different answers can be given in various cases.

To attribute religious celibacy to a person's feeling more or less at home in that style of life, the second objection goes, is irreligious. Where are all those lofty reasons traditionally assigned as motives for religious celibacy? Celibacy is for the sake of the kingdom of God and for the following of Christ in the form of life which he chose for himself and recommended to his disciples. Liberating a person, it leads to greater love of God and neighbor, and it facilitates apostolic action and pastoral care. It consecrates a person to God, Christ, Church, and ministry in a new, special, distinctive way. It bears witness to the transcendence of the kingdom of God and to the new life in the Spirit which begins now in time and will be fully actualized in eternity. It also signifies the union of the Church with her one spouse, Christ. These reasons gleaned from Church documents[1]—are not they the reasons why celibate life is chosen?

Some of these traditional reasons, perhaps all of them, are included in anyone's feeling comfortable with celibate life. They indicate partially what the celibate is satisfied with. But what ultimately prompts the choice of religious celibacy and enables these traditional reasons to function as actual motives is a person's feeling rela-

---

1–Vatican Council II, *Dogmatic Constitution on the Church*, no. 44; *Decree on the Appropriate Renewal of Religious Life*, no. 12; *Decree on Priestly Ministry and Life*, no. 16; Second Synod of Bishops, *The Ministerial Priesthood*, pt. 2, sec. I, no. 4.

tively at ease and fulfilled in celibate life. Reasons, after
all, are in the order of intelligence. Intelligence guides
the direction which choices take, but intelligence does not
make the choices. Choices are made by the will, and the
will is moved by the good. Celibate life is chosen because
it appears to be good, that is, satisfying, comfortable,
promising. It appears so because of one or several reasons
grasped by the mind but most critically because of satisfaction, comfort, and hope actually experienced or felt
while preparing for or living a celibate dedication. There
are people who understand the reasons for celibacy, who
are even attracted to the values represented by these
reasons, but who are in no way inclined to adopt that
style of life. The critical factor is that they do not feel it,
in fact or in anticipation, as satisfying, comfortable, or
promising. So we have drawn the conclusion that **the**
reason why a person chooses religious celibacy is that
he or she feels comfortable in that way of life, even
though it involves difficulties.

Then the question arises: Why does a person feel
comfortable with celibacy? The answer is to be found
in his or her personality and life history. Basic factors
are inherited bodily constitution and psychic temperament. Then there is character formed in the course of
life at home and later in school and society. Family life
and relations to different members of the family last-
ingly influence outlook on life and values. Neighborhood
environment and early playmates make their impres-
sions, as do school surroundings and classmates. Various
talents are developed and interests awakened, depending on environment and education. At different stages
emerge "significant others" who influence life's direction. Special friendships play a developmental role. All
along the way are unique interior experiences which
shape a person's vision and values. These and perhaps
other factors accumulate to make a particular person

at some point feel that religious celibacy is a more or less satisfying way of life.

Among the many factors leading to the choice of celibacy may be attraction to one or another or several of the traditional reasons for that way of life. The attraction is not usually to abstract ideas but to examples, that is, some known priests or religious brothers or sisters, or to imaginative daydreams of self as priest or sister or brother. Sometimes these traditional reasons may be misinterpreted when envisioned in living examples or dreams of the future. For instance, one may imagine celibacy as freedom from many cares, not discerning that, paradoxically, to sustain celibacy's freedom from certain cares, one depends greatly on the support of others and is not free from cares to ensure that support. If such misinterpretation has played a major role in leading one to adopt religious celibacy, one may have considerable difficulty in adjusting to that way of life when a quite different reality is discovered. But such a discovery need not lead to rejecting religious celibacy, for many other factors also may be influential in its choice.

Some factors which coalesce to incline a person to the celibate way of life may be neurotic, but such factors need not be present. Even when some are, still others are perfectly sound. If the neurotic factors do not impede peaceful and productive life and acceptable social behavior and relationships, the undertaking of celibacy is not neurotic, any more than the slight neuroses which everyone possesses render the choice of marriage neurotic. If the neurotic factors do hinder the values mentioned, then the person is not fit for celibacy any more than he or she is fit for marriage. If a seriously debilitating neurosis is discovered after entering upon the celibate way of life, it must be treated just as if such a neurotic condition were discovered after marriage.

Religious celibacy, moreover, is rarely, if ever, chosen

in isolation from other values. It is chosen as one element in a greater whole. For example, a man chooses religious celibacy as a condition of the diaconate or priesthood whose ministry he desires; or a woman chooses religious celibacy as one element of religious life entailing also a particular community and specific apostolic service through prayer and action.

The choice of celibacy, then, issues from an incredibly complex confluence of forces in the course of a lifetime. The believing Christian sees this growing stream of influences as falling within God's abiding care for his creatures and constituting a vocation to the celibate life. God's call to celibacy comes in the form of one's personal history. To hear that call is to be sensitive to who one is, and to discern one's own desires—to know one's self. To answer the call is to accept one's self. Celibacy is the renunciation of several things, but not of self. It is saying yes to the person one is as a result of one's history which has been in God's hands.

Celibacy, then, is a gift before it is a choice or commitment. It is first a gift because it issues from personal history which is not entirely of one's own making. No one selects his or her basic temperament or the fundamental orientation of his or her personality by parents. Many other influences of life are not chosen but simply given. Some influences are chosen, of course, and the impact of others freely accepted, but most of these choices are at least partially conditioned by unwilled and even unknown factors. In any case, the freely chosen influences constitute only some of the factors which now prompt one to adopt or continue celibate life. The initial or continuing choice of celibacy is the acceptance of a gift—one's self as the culmination of one's personal history unfolded under God's care.

Because the vocation to celibacy is as complex as a person's whole life, the choice of celibacy is never fully explainable, even by the celibate making the choice. Not even several reasons, much less one reason, adequately account for it. The choice of celibacy always remains mysterious, not only to others, but to celibates themselves. They can unearth reasons for it by reflecting on their lives, and they may be able to pinpoint the major influences which led to the choice, but it would take years of psychiatric analysis to comprehend all the influences. Even with lengthy depth analysis it is doubtful that such comprehension could be achieved. Even if it were, mystery would still remain, for there would be the question why this person was the subject of that particular confluence of forces leading to the present choice of celibacy. Celibacy entails the very mystery of one's own existence.

Similar statements can be made about marriage. Why one marries at all and why one marries this individual rather than another are rooted in personal history. Husbands and wives can give reasons why they have chosen their partners, but the reasons seem shallow when enunciated. The reasons are true, but they fall short of explaining fully why these marriages were entered into and now endure. The fact is that two people, at certain points in their long and complex personal histories shaped by many factors, found themselves liking each other, comfortable with each other, to the extent that they were moved to choose to live their lives together. The personal histories of a couple constitute, in the eyes of faith, their vocation to marriage and to this marriage. Choice of a marriage is an acceptance of self as a gift, as well as acceptance of another.

Now we can discern some answers to the questions raised at the beginning of these reflections. Efforts to discover convincing and moving reasons for celibacy are so often unsatisfactory because of the dispositions of those to whom they are proposed. Those who do not have a personal history disposing them for celibacy, or who have such a disposition but are not in touch with their deeper selves, will not find persuasive any reasons offered for celibacy. Those who have such a personal history and are at one with themselves will find the reasons unsatisfactory because they will be aware, at least confusedly, that the reasons do not adequately and ultimately explain why they have chosen celibacy. They have a sense of choosing celibacy for many deeper and more subtle reasons, though they cannot articulate them. People partially comfortable and partially uncomfortable with celibacy or only partially in tune to themselves will, at one moment, sense no power in the reasons and, at another moment, feel faintly their force; thus they remain perplexed about the value of celibacy for themselves.

The reasons usually adduced for celibacy are inadequate to explain **fully** any particular person's choice of celibacy. They frequently play a role in a person's choice of celibacy but, compared to all the other influences at work, their role is partial and dependent on many of the other influences for their effectiveness. At least a dim awareness of the gap between a half-dozen general reasons for celibacy and the mysterious, complex multiplicity of influences behind one's own actual or future choice of celibacy explains why discussions about celibacy are so often unsatisfying. These discussions, moreover, tend to deal in generalities, while celibacy is ultimately a personal mystery, which is scarcely touched by abstract propositions and never explained by arguments. More satisfying than discussions of celibacy are testimonies of personal celibate experience. These testimonies portray in concrete form the value of celibacy, thus providing for the appearance of the good and so giving others the opportunity to discern if they are, or are not, comfortable with that good.

The difficulty of justifying celibacy points to the ultimately personal, mysterious, and gift quality of the celibate way of life. This statement is no claim to some special prerogative for celibacy. Similar difficulty would be experienced in any attempt to justify actual choices of marriage. But to be aware that celibacy is a personal mysterious gift enables one to look in the right place for an answer when seeking to determine whether or not one should be a religious celibate. The answer is not going to come in the shape of fully convincing reasons withstanding debate in the public forum. It is going to come from self-awareness and sensitive perception of one's own deepest, enduring inclinations and attractions. It is, moreover, not going to remove all uncertainty and all risk-taking. We never fathom the depths of our own selves. The choice of celibacy will always entail hope in God. Awareness of celibacy as a personal mysterious gift also makes it possible to lead people by appropriate means to adopt the celibate way of life. Those means are not reasons or arguments for celibacy but attractive celibate lives and the testimony of those who live them.

Finally, so much more effort is invested in attempting to justify celibacy than in legitimizing marriage because religious celibacy is an unusual way of life, though not unnatural. The number of religious celibates in the world population is not immense, and in some cultures none exist. Celibates as an unusual species are bound to raise people's curiosity and to provoke the question of why their celibacy. Even celibates, conscious of following an unusual path, ask themselves the question. Attempts are made to answer the question, not by the testimony of personal histories and careful listening to what is said, but by explanation and understanding, that is, by reasons for celibacy. But because of the nature of celibacy as the outcome of a mysterious complex of influences over a lifetime, the reasons offered never appear satisfying to speaker or audience. So other reasons are proposed, only to be found wanting. Thus celibacy is forever being justified.

Do the reasons offered for celibacy, then, have any value? Earlier in this chapter we listed the traditional reasons for celibacy as gleaned from Church documents. Are we saying now that they are worthless? No. They are valid in two ways: first, as explanations of why the Church accepts celibate life in some of its members and, secondly, as partial justification for individuals' celibacy. The remainder of this chapter will consider the first of these ways of being valid. In the next chapter we will look at the second way.

From early Christian times, some Christians have felt the desire to dedicate themselves entirely to religious concerns in a celibate way of life. Given the infinitely diverse personal histories of millions of Christians through the centuries, it is not surprising that some men and women have felt this way. How should the Church react to this wish of some of its members? Should the Church brand it as a temptation to violate God's will expressed in the inclination of men and women to unite as two in one flesh? Should celibate life be declared disobedience to God's command, recorded in Genesis, to be fruitful and multiply?

Answers opposing celibacy have flourished at times among some groups of Christians. But on the whole the Church has been sensitive to its members who have preferred a religiously oriented life through celibacy. Rather than condemn their desire, it has sought to help them incorporate the fulfillment of their wish into Christian discipleship. It has accepted celibacy for the sake of the kingdom, that is, celibacy undertaken for the purpose of contributing to the realization of God's will in his creation.

It follows that "for the sake of the kingdom" is simply

a reason for choosing celibacy, a motive which must inspire celibacy, if that celibacy is to be a Christian style of life. It is not a reason for choosing celibacy in preference to other styles of Christian life, for they too must be for the sake of the kingdom. The difference between the various styles of Christian life is not in one's being for the sake of the kingdom and the others not being so, but in the diverse spheres of life in which each seeks that God's will be done on earth as in heaven.

Another reason explaining the Church's acceptance of celibacy is its enabling a person to follow Christ in the form of life he chose for himself and recommended to his disciples. Confronted by the desire of some of its members to live celibately for the sake of the kingdom, the Church could accept their desire as authentically Christian because of its conviction that Christ himself had so lived. The Church also saw Jesus' recommending celibacy in his words recorded in Matthew's Gospel: "Some men are incapable of sexual activity from birth; some have been deliberately made so; and some there are who have freely renounced sex for the sake of God's reign. Let him accept this teaching who can" (Matt. 19:12).

Some biblical exegetes today propose that, in view of the context in which these words are found, Jesus is not recommending celibacy here. He is indicating, rather, the demand which the kingdom of God makes on a person whose marriage fails. Whether or not Jesus recommended celibacy verbally at some time is relatively unimportant. Neither is it terribly important whether or not he ever explicitly chose celibacy, that is, explicitly made a promise or vow to God to live celibately; for we can discern in his life at least an implicit choice of celibacy in the way he sought to realize in his personal life the reign of his Father. His conduct can be interpreted as a recommendation of celibacy by example. There is sufficient basis for the Church to acknowledge celibate life as a legitimate form of Christian discipleship.

A third reason offered for celibacy is that it liberates the heart from earthly cares and from obstacles which might impede the fervor of charity and perfection of worship. The Church's mission is to serve Christ's liberation of men and women from enslavement to the perishable, weak, finite, and sinful concerns of humanity alienated from God. Celibacy for the sake of the kingdom, an authentic following of Christ, realizes some measure of freedom from this bondage. The Church therefore accepts celibate life as partial accomplishment of its mission.

Liberation from earthly cares and potential obstacles to fervent charity and perfect worship should not be construed simply as freedom from the cares of marriage and family. Christ did not come to free us from any human responsibilities, but from sin and death. He came to heal human life and enrich it with God's grace. Hence he points out our responsibilities and intensifies our sense of them and our concern for one another, society, and all creation. What he frees us from is enslavement to humanity separated from God. In Christian marriage Christ frees men and women from enslavement to marital and family concerns precisely as severed from God. The Church recognizes that in celibacy too Christ frees from such bondage by inspiring renunciation of marriage and family, rather than by sanctifying them in the sacrament of matrimony.

The Church's mission is to serve Christ's gift of ever greater love of God and neighbor in his members—that special love which the New Testament calls **agape.** In celibacy the Church discerns a sign, occasion, and means of Christ's intensifying that love. Those who choose celibacy for the sake of the kingdom manifest greater love of God and neighbor, not necessarily greater love than someone else's, but greater than that which they themselves once had. The process of making up one's mind to choose celibacy initially, or to reaffirm a previous choice, is an occasion of growth in the love of God and neighbor, perhaps not beyond that of anybody else, but beyond one's own previous measure. One's celibacy is an enduring reminder to devote self more wholeheartedly to God and neighbor in whatever sphere of life one moves, so that by means of it Christ stimulates growth in love of God and neighbor, at least in comparison to one's own prior degree of love. Because of celibacy's relationship to growth in the love of God and neighbor, the Church accepts it as a way of life which partially accomplishes its mission in the world. Other ways of life, of course, can also be signs, occasions, and means of Christ's bestowal of greater charity.

A fifth reason for celibacy is that it facilitates apostolic activity and pastoral care. The Church can rely on celibates to undertake ministries which married men and women could accept only with difficulty or not at all. One Protestant minister tells of his first pastorate in a decaying area of a major city. He could not, in conscience, have his wife and child live in the area for safety and health reasons. Therefore he had to live outside the area, which, he admits, hampered his ministry and his effectiveness with the people.

Celibates generally can move from one locality to another more quickly and with less difficulty and expense than married people. They have fewer possessions to be transported. With less property, they are not so legally involved in a locale. They do not have to root children up from familiar neighborhoods and schools and then be concerned about their integration into new ones.

Celibacy does not guarantee, of course, that a particular person is more available to a wider range of people than some men and women in other ways of life.

Not every celibate spends more time and energy than some non-celibate people on certain activities vital to the Church's mission, such as preaching, conducting worship, teaching, supervising charitable works. But because at least sometimes and even often, in some measure, celibacy does in fact facilitate apostolic action and pastoral care, the Church welcomes it as a way of life for those members who wish it.

In the expression of the last two reasons for celibacy, the adverbial phrase **with undivided heart** or **in an undivided way** is occasionally added: celibacy is a means to greater love of God with undivided heart; celibacy fosters the apostolate in an undivided way. These phrases echo St. Paul's exhortation to the Corinthians: "The unmarried man is busy with the Lord's affairs, concerned with pleasing the Lord, but the married man is busy with the world's demands and occupied with pleasing his wife. This means he is divided" (I Cor. 7:32-33). Paul writes the same thing about the virgin and the married woman.

This idea of undividedness in love or apostolic dedication must be carefully interpreted. God is never an object of love apart from other objects of love, in particular, spouse and children. God is loved concommitantly with others insofar as they are truly loved only in God. The First Letter of John, moreover, stresses that there is no love of God without simultaneous love of neighbor (3:17; 4:12, 20-21). There is only one Christian love, or **agape,** charity; by it both God and neighbor are loved together (St. Thomas Aquinas, **Summa theologiae,** II-II, q. 25, a. 1). In addition, in Christian marriage, **agape** penetrates, purifies, and incorporates into its own thrust toward God all other kinds of loving acts. Christian marriage, therefore, like celibacy, tends toward love of God in an undivided way. Celibates, moreover, have other people in their lives whom they must love; they too must love them with the same **agape** by which they love God and assimilate other kinds of love into their charity.

To say that celibacy provides for undivided dedication to the apostolate or pastoral care whereas Christian marriage does not, is to ignore one or the other of two facts. It may overlook the fact that celibates too have mundane affairs to be cared for, like meals, laundry, shopping, housecleaning, recreation, friendships, and aged parents' welfare. Or it may be blind to the fact that in developing marital love, rearing children, and building a just world, men and women are carrying out the apostolic mission of the Church, as Vatican Council II eloquently stated in **Dogmatic Constitution on the Church** (chap. 4) and **Decree on the Apostolate of the Laity.**

So the phrase **with undivided heart** or **in an undivided way** is not meant to contrast what celibacy assures and other ways of Christian life do not. Rather, they signify the quality of the love and of the apostolic or pastoral devotion which should be found in a Christian, whatever the condition of his or her life. St. Paul's statements are open to many exceptions. They could be true of specific celibate and married people, all factors of their lives being taken into account. Evidently Paul believed they were true for many or most of the people he knew at Corinth. Although celibacy is not the only means of fostering undivided love and apostolic dedication, it does foster them; and so the Church accepts celibate life.

A sixth reason offered for celibacy is that it consecrates a person **more intimately, under a new title, in a new way, in a special way,** to the service of God and neighbor. The Church understandably accepts a way of life which entails a person's dedicating self to God's and humanity's service more thoroughly than previously and confirming that dedication in some public expression of it before the Christian community. Of course, a Christian couple entering sacramental marriage similarly conse-

crate themselves; they are henceforth more intimately
united to God through the sacrament of matrimony
and strive to serve God and fellow human beings under
a new title, in a new and special way. The distinctive consecration which celibacy involves makes it different
from, though not necessarily better than, the distinctive
consecration of marriage, and also makes it acceptable
to the Church as a legitimate way of life.

A seventh reason for celibacy is its value as witness
or sign. This reason appears most frequently in the documents from which we have been gathering motives for
celibacy. Expressions of this reason vary according to
that to which celibacy points. Celibacy bears witness to
the transcendence of the kingdom of God, the kingdom's
overriding necessity in comparison to earthly considerations, the radical character of the Gospel, the presence
of the Absolute God inviting men and women to life with
him, and union with Christ as the final, absolute good.
In an age when sex is exaggerated, celibacy recalls men
and women to faithful love and reveals the ultimate
meaning of life. Celibacy announces heavenly goods, the
new and eternal life, and the freedom of the children of
God which are already our possession in virtue of Christ's
redemption. Celibacy testifies to the surpassing power of
Christ the King and of the Holy Spirit. It indicates the
spiritual quality of the generative power, the fruitfulness
of the New Law, and the pastoral activity of the Church.
It points forward to the resurrected life which is to come,
where "they neither marry nor are given in marriage,
but live like angels in heaven" (Matt. 22:30). Finally,
celibacy signifies, not simply the union of Christ and his
Church, but the Church's union with Christ alone.

If we consider carefully Christian marriage with the
love which animates it and the indissolubility and unity
which characterize it, and if we consider the difficulty of
living fully Christian married life in today's world, we

can discern in well-lived Christian marriage some testimony to most of the things which celibacy is said to signify. Celibacy remains, however, a particularly powerful witness because of its relative rarity; a celibate on the scene usually raises more questions in people's minds than a married or single person.

In God's covenant with Israel, revelation of his love is frequently communicated through the imagery of marriage. That imagery is still forceful in conveying the meaning of God's grace in Christ. But the Church has recognized that the celibate life desired by some of its members also testifies to that grace clearly and strikingly. Therefore the Church readily accepts celibacy as complementing the witness of Christian marriage in the ecclesial mission of declaring to the world the bounteous grace of God.

The familiar reasons for celibacy, then, explain quite persuasively the Church's acceptance of celibacy among its members. But these reasons also explain validly, though partially, why individuals choose celibacy, as we will see in the next chapter.

Chapter 2

MOTIVES FOR CELIBACY

That the reasons traditionally offered for celibacy are valid as partial motivation for someone's choice of celibacy is my conviction resulting from reflection on my own experience and the role which the reasons for celibacy have played in my life.

Celibacy, for example, is claimed to be liberating. I have found that it has liberated me for a considerable amount of teaching theology, research in that field, writing for the religious press, theological lecturing, preaching, retreat work, sacramental ministry, spiritual counseling, liturgical prayer, and related activities. If we regard these activities as among the multitude of apostolic activities in which Christians engage, I can say that celibacy has liberated me for a considerable amount of particular kinds of apostolic activity — an amount which I would not have accomplished if I had been married.

When I look back over my life, I feel quite certain that if I had been married and with a family, I could not have accomplished the quantity of these kinds of apostolic work which in fact I have achieved. Perhaps someone else could have done as much and still have been married. I speak only for myself. If I had been married, I simply would not have had the time and energy for all that in fact I have done. I would have had to devote some of my time and energy to caring for wife and children; with the remaining time and energy I would not have been able to accompish the work I have done, given the caliber of my native talent.

I have had to give some of my resources to caring for my religious community, my friends, and the family of my origin. But the time and energy expended on these people have not been as great as what I would have had to devote to wife and especially to children. As adults, these people could attend to their own basic needs, unlike small or young children. Interaction with adults, moreover, is more efficient than dealing with children, especially when they are very young. Community members, friends, family, and I mutually understand, finally, that in our relationships normally a high priority will be given to our respective Christian ministries; we are not readily going to be offended if one or the other leaves for some time to fulfill his or her ministry. With community members especially, I meet in the understanding that a purpose of our community is precisely to foster and support one another's apostolic activity.

It will have been noticed that so far we have been talking about the amount or quantity of apostolic work for which celibacy has liberated me. We should note now that the liberation has been for certain kinds of apostolic action. We have not said that celibacy frees for apostolic activity without qualification. Making a Christian marriage work and developing a Christian family is apostolic, that is, integral to the Church's mission to convey the message and grace of Christ to all humanity. Celibacy has liberated me from the kinds of apostolic activity proper to Christian marriage, so that I could dedicate myself to other kinds of apostolic activity in a measure that would not have been possible if I had also had to attend to the activities characteristic of Christian marriage.

Nor is it being said that married persons could not also perform some of these apostolic activities in which I have been engaged, or even all of them if Church discipline allowed. It is affirmed simply that in fact I have been freed by celibacy to accomplish an amount of certain kinds of apostolic work which I believe I would not have been able to do if I had been married.

It has not necessarily been morally better for me to have dedicated myself more to certain kinds of apostolic effort rather than to have chosen Christian marriage and to have done less in the line in which I have been productive. But since I esteem the tasks to which I have devoted myself as critically important for the Church, humanity, and God's reign, celibacy's freeing me for them to the maximum of my resources justifies partially but really, within my value system, my choice of celibate life.

Have I lost something of my humanity in being free from bearing responsibilities for wife and children? No doubt I have. But I also have fulfilled my human potential in certain respects to a degree I would not have fulfilled it if I had borne those marital and family responsibilities. Moreover, since I value highly those activities for the sake of which I have foregone marriage and family, I do not feel unduly deprived or impoverished.

Besides, celibacy has not freed me of responsibilities for those with whom I live, work, pray, and play, and for all men and women. On the contrary, I believe that celibacy has helped me to become more aware of the responsibilities which we all have to those to whom we are related beyond the circle of our own kin by blood and marriage. When I perceive the protectiveness and defensiveness which understandably appear in some husbands' and fathers' attitudes toward their families vis-à-vis the rest of the world, I wonder if in marriage I would have arrived at the sense of broader responsibilities which I have gained in celibate life. The often-heard assertion that celibacy frees from responsibilities is a myth. Celibacy does not free from responsibilities without qualification; rather, it frees from certain responsibilities, leaves others standing, and imposes new ones.

Another reason offered for celibacy is that it leads to greater love of God and neighbor. As I look back over my life, I can see that my celibacy has promoted greater love of God and neighbor, not in comparison to someone else's love, but in comparison to my own previous measures of love. By a strong innate drive, I have always been intellectually curious and since my late teens, fascinated by ultimate questions about life, the world, God. A prominent strain running through my life has been a search for answers to these kinds of questions. This strong interest is undoubtedly one of the factors in my personal history disposing me to celibate life. Celibacy has provided me with time and energy to pursue my quest in the study of philosophy, Scripture, theology, and the sciences of man, in mental prayer, and in simply thinking about the mystery of human existence. As a result, my habitual awareness of God has grown over the years and my choices are made with greater consciousness of him as their ultimate end. He has become a genuine personal presence in my life. My relationship to him is the milieu in which all my other personal relationships flourish.

With ever-growing clarity I have seen that this relationship to God is inseparable from love of neighbor, whether man or woman, black or white, rich or poor, young or old, virtuous or sinner. I have become increasingly impressed by the words of I John 4:20: "One who has no love for the brother he has seen cannot love the God he has not seen." Personal, social, and cultural factors—some of which I am aware, some not—still enslave me, hindering my loving God with all my heart, soul, strength, and mind, and loving my neighbor as myself. But the vision of what should be has become clearer and more persistent, the imperative more felt, the appropriate response more likely.

Perhaps I could have grown in love of God and neighbor just as much or more in marriage. But that is not the point. The point is that my celibacy has contributed to my growth in love of God and neighbor. Other elements in my life have contributed to that growth, of course, but so has my celibacy as a condition of my life which has allowed and prompted activities leading to greater love of God and neighbor. In view of what has come to pass with regard to my love of God and neighbor in the course of my celibate life, it makes sense to me to continue in this way of life. I can see growth in the love of God and neighbor as truly a partial reason for my continuing to choose celibacy.

On the other hand, I do not believe that I would cease to grow in love of God and neighbor were I to choose another style of life. That belief, however, derives at least part of its firmness precisely because of the growth which has already been achieved in my celibate life. The conviction derives also from a greater appreciation of the possibilities for growth in the love of God and neighbor inherent in Christian marriage—an appreciation I did not have when I initially chose the celibate style of life. Because I did not have that appreciation twenty-five years ago, I suspect that I may very well not have taken advantage of those possibilities had I then chosen marriage rather than celibate life. There is all the more reason, then, for my finding celibacy's promotion of love of God and neighbor to be genuinely a partial justification for my choice of celibacy.

Still another reason given for celibacy is its facilitating apostolic and pastoral ministry. As mentioned above in the consideration of celibacy as liberating, celibacy has promoted such activity in my life in the sense of having enabled me to devote more of my time, talent, and energy to certain endeavors necessary in the mission of the Church. As a result I have done more in these areas than I would have done if I had been married. Celibacy, then, in my case, has facilitated quantitatively certain kinds of apostolic and pastoral work. But has it facilitated such action qualitatively? Has it enabled me to be a better preacher, a better confessor, or better anything else than I would have been if I had been married?

Celibacy has liberated me from certain concerns which very likely would have hampered the quality of apostolic and pastoral work—concerns such as family quarrels, sickness of children, or a rebellious teen-age son or daughter. But comparable concerns have had their place in my celibate life—distracting disagreements with superiors, mortal illness of a parent, friends' needs. However, dealing with such difficulties may be in the long run a source of growth as much as an interference in the quality of one's ministry.

Striving to live celibately has resulted in some inhibition in regard to expressing feelings and emotions. This inhibition surely has cut down on the quality of some apostolic and pastoral functions, for example, presiding over the liturgy, preaching, socializing. But celibacy itself has not been the only cause of this reluctance, which, moreover, has not always dominated and has been overcome to some degree. Besides, the striving to live celibately contributed at least partially to inhibition because of some early misconceptions about celibacy rather than because of the celibacy itself. I doubt that authentic celibacy by itself, without other factors in play, inevitably hampers the quality of apostolic and pastoral action.

But is it possible for me as a celibate to counsel adequately—in homily, in writing, in private conversation—husbands, wives, parents, and children? I am not living in the intimacy of the husband-wife relationship or in the context of a family. How can I minister to those living in these situations when I do not have the same experience?

The answer to this question is not a simple "I can" or "I cannot." Much depends on what advice I am expected to give. I am capable of informing married people, parents, children, widows, divorced people what ideals the Gospel and the Church hold up for them in their situations in life. I may not be able to appreciate from within, so to speak, the difficulties which those ideas present, the limited alternatives for living them, the enormity of the struggle required to follow them; but I can present the ideals. My ability to do this depends not on my having these people's experiences but on my knowledge of the Gospel, the Church's teaching, and theology.

I can do more than present ideals. I can help these people in their response to them. I can engage people in dialogue to help them to understand accurately the ideals, clarify their own difficulties with them, discern carefully the alternative ways of living them, and courageously face the struggles required. My aim is not to make decisions for them but to help them make their own decisions in the light of the Gospel as read and interpreted by the living Church. My ability to do this sort of thing depends more upon my skill in counseling than upon my having their experiences.

That no one can counsel another person without having that person's experience is a claim requiring qualifications. Much depends on the counselor's knowledge of the aspect of life for which help is sought and on his or her skill in the art of counseling. The counselor's sensitivity to, and respect for, the dignity, intelligence, freedom, good will, and suffering of the one seeking help are important factors to take into account. Counseling skill is sharpened by dealing with a wide range of many people's problems rather than with a few problems in one's own life. Only out of numerous similar cases might some possible helps be derived for a particular case which will never be identical with any other people's problems, including the counselor's own. Celibacy of itself does not prevent anyone from counseling another.

In one way my celibacy has promoted qualitatively better apostolic and pastoral activity of certain kinds—again, not better than any one else's but better than my own previous activity. Insofar as my celibacy has led to my growth in love of God and neighbor and has freed time and energy for more study of, and prayerful reflection on, the Gospel, it has improved the Christian spirit in which I have engaged in certain apostolic and pastoral tasks. That improved spirit surely has some influence on the quality of those actions. I may have developed the same spirit in marriage, but I do not know that. All that I can say, and all that is significant here, is that for me celibacy has in fact improved my apostolic and pastoral work.

Celibacy has fostered my apostolic and pastoral efforts, both quantatively and qualitatively, in a more involved way as a result of the freedom which it has provided. Many times in the course of my celibate life I have been very much conscious of my not having many responsibilities which husbands and fathers have, and of not having to spend amounts of time and energy caring for the food, shelter, clothing, education, and other needs of wife and children in today's complex society. Heightened consciousness of this freedom has poignantly raised the question in my mind about my purpose in life, my achievements, my contribution to the human race, my country, the Church. Am I copping out?

In those moments of awareness and questioning, I have seen the magnitude of my responsibilities for aspects of life for which married people or others are perhaps less directly responsible. I have seen my obligation to devote myself generously to prayer, to study of the Gospel, to preaching and writing, to championing causes which need to be promoted but may very well be lost sight of or feared by most of those with big life-investments in the status quo upon which support and welfare of wife and children depend. I have been inspired to give more energy and time to activities like prayer and retreats which would help me grow in love of God and neighbor, or at least grow in my awareness of the need for greater love of God and neighbor. I have been inspired to be more conscientious about certain apostolic and pastoral works, to spend myself more generously on them, to fill more of my time with them.

I can conceive of marriage and family as facilitating better apostolic and pastoral work. Wife and children could supply support, inspiration, recreation, and fulfillment of personal needs to sustain me in day to day work, in difficult projects, or in prolonged ones. It would give a background of experience creating sensitivity and sympathy for certain problems of those to whom I minister. As a celibate, however, I can gain some of this help from community, friends, and relatives. Marriage, moreover, does not guarantee the presence of such aid any more than celibacy assures its total absence.

Celibacy's being for the sake of the kingdom of God—another reason offered for celibacy—has motivated my choice of celibacy in two ways. First it has influenced the kind of celibate life I have chosen, namely, a positive rather than a negative one. From time to time over the years I have wondered about my celibate life. Was it worth the deprivations it entailed and the struggles it sometimes demanded? In those questioning moments I often realized that my celibacy is not a negative quality; it is not a not-being-married or a not-being-husband-and-father. It is a positive reality, a life for the sake of God's reign, a life dedicated to the coming of his kingdom in humanity and creation. Marriage and parenthood are also for that purpose in their own way, but celibacy too is for that end in its own way. From this realization came the inspiration to invest myself more wholeheartedly in those activities for which my celibacy frees me and which are the professed purposes of the religious community and the priesthood to which I belong. I quit moping around feeling lonely, for example, and put my mind to composing a homily or writing an article or meditating.

Secondly, celibacy's being for the sake of the kingdom has influenced my choice of that style of life over marriage or some other way of life. This influence is not based on the idea that other ways of Christian life are not for the sake of the kingdom, although I admit that I may have been determined by such an idea in my youth—an idea that was and still is widespread. But if **for the sake of the kingdom** is understood in the sense of **for the sake of the kingdom to be realized in certain kinds of Christian activity,** then for the sake of the kingdom I have chosen celibacy rather than marriage or another style of Christian life. From my early days I have desired to preside over the Eucharist, to confer the sacraments, to preach, to help people follow Christ—in a word, to serve the actualization of the kingdom of God in these ways. In the discipline and custom of the Roman Catholic Church, most of these particular ways of realizing God's reign have been allotted to celibates. I therefore chose celibacy in order to engage in these specific activities. Though the Church's discipline is changing, it has done so only slightly, so I continue to choose celibacy as a means of working for the kingdom in these particular ways.

Another reason offered for celibacy is to follow Christ in the form of life he chose for himself. Occasionally this reason has motivated my **continuing** choice of celibacy.

When I have felt the difficulties of celibacy, sometimes I have consoled myself with the thought that Jesus lived a comparable life, that he too must have experienced the want of a wife's presence with love, care, and encouragement; he too must have missed the satisfaction and joy of seeing his own offspring. Yet in his dedication to, and absorption in, the mission to which he felt himself called, he accepted these deprivations. I too can bear them gracefully and profitably if I give myself wholeheartedly to my mission.

On the other hand, that Jesus recommended celibacy to his disciples was a partial reason for my initial choice of celibacy. That reason was wrapped up in a particular exegesis of Matthew's Gospel, chapter 19, verses 10-12, and in a theology of the evangelical counsels, of the vows to follow them, and of Christian perfection as life's goal. I suspect it was the latter notion of Christian perfection as life's goal which made the primary appeal to me in my youthful hopefulness about life. Such hope is common to young people whose optimism about human life has not yet been tempered by experience and by knowledge of history. The evangelical counsels as recommendations of Christ over and above the call of duty, and the vows to keep them, appeared as concrete steps toward a full Christian life. To choose vowed celibacy on the basis of a recommendation by no one less than Jesus made sense in the context of desire for a complete Christian life.

If I had any idea that celibacy and the vow of celibacy would make me more perfectly Christian than marriage would, that idea was soon dissipated by instruction that celibacy and its vow were only a means to a profoundly Christian life, not Christian perfection itself. That perfection consists in love of God and neighbor available to anyone in any way of life. Nevertheless, until I had a different and better understanding of Christian life generally and Christian marriage in particular, as well as experience with religious life and celibacy, I did think that the possibilities for an authentic Christian life inherent in celibacy were superior to the possibilities inherent in marriage.

In recent years I have found another exegesis of St. Matthew's Gospel more likely, namely, that Jesus is there recommending, not celibacy, but foregoing remarriage after the failure of a marriage. I see more clearly the instrumental nature of the evangelical counsels and vows to pursue them, though I also appreciate from experience the genuine help the fulfillment of the evangelical counsels and their vows can be for growth in Christian love of God and neighbor. My concept of Christian marriage, however, now definitely includes following the evangelical counsels in a way appropriate to that style of life. So an explicit recommendation of celibacy by Jesus is not the explanation for my choice of celibate life today.

A new, special, or distinctive consecration to God, Christ, and the Church is sometimes offered as reason for celibacy. I now understand "new, special, distinctive" consecration to mean, not necessarily a better consecration, but a different one in addition to any other consecration that may exist, for example, that of baptism. Christian marriage vows are also a new, special, distinctive consecration. Earlier in my celibate life, when I saw celibacy in the context mentioned above and when my idea of Christian marriage was impoverished, I suspect that I saw the new, special, and distinctive consecration attributed to celibacy as involving a superior consecration over that of marriage, so that it was a partial reason for my initial choice of celibacy.

The vow of celibacy as a distinctive consecration in the sense of a personal free commitment in my life has been a very powerful partial reason for my continuing to choose celibate life. At times I have found myself

uncertain about my life as celibate. I have stabilized
myself by going back, so to speak, to that decision expressed in my vow and to the life-project which that
decision embodied. Whoever or whatever else I was, I
was one who had said yes to God about trying to live
celibate life as a positive, love-filled, useful, even exciting way of life. If good reasons existed for no longer aim-
ing at that goal, God would understand and not hold me
to it. But at the moment of uncertainty, the first step
was to say yes again for that day in continuity with the
first yes. Anchored in the original declaration of intention for my life, I could seek resolutions for whatever
was upsetting. More than once my continuing choice of
celibate life has been based on the fact that the vow of
celibacy is a distinctive consecration in the sense of a
very personal free decision which I once made about how
I wished to live for God and Christ.

Left for consideration are reasons for celibacy based
on its being a sign of one or another mystery: the transcendence of God's kingdom, the new life in the Spirit
available to men and women in time, that life in its
heavenly fulfillment, and the union of the Church with
her one spouse, Christ. Of these reasons for celibacy
only the first two have been partial reasons for my choice
of celibate life.

I believe that the goal of creation and human striving
is that God's will be done on earth as it is in heaven, as
we frequently pray. The consummation of the universe,
the ultimate happiness of all men and women, and my
fulfillment are realized by God's will being done in the
universe and in us human beings. If there is anything
worth saying, it is that. A most powerful demonstration
of this belief is celibacy chosen as an affirmation that
God's reign is a higher value than any other values, even
the most marvelous value of human love between man
and woman. In a secularized culture, especially one in

which it is assumed that marriage or at least physical sexual activity is inevitable, I think that it is worthwhile to be celibate and thus provoke men and women to inquire why, to wonder what motivates such a choice, to ask what Reality and Value can override the realities and values which are assumed to be the only ones.

I also believe that all too many men and women in our culture have a poor idea of what love between man and woman is, and what love between man and man, woman and woman is. More often than not, as dialogues in novels, short stories, films, and plays testify, the word **love** means predominantly and sometimes exclusively mutual physical sexual pleasure. Yet human love is much more than that, as Harry Stack Sullivan, Rollo May, Erich Fromm and others concerned with men's and women's well-being keep reminding us. If more marriages are to endure and enrich spouses, if single people are to find genuinely human fulfillment in relationships with the opposite or same sex, a better idea of human love must be lived and broadcast.

Women today are rejecting the shackles of oppression by men. They are revolting against, among other things, men's exploitation of them as "sex objects." But all too often in their striving, instead of rising to the dignity of being free persons and drawing men with them up to the same dignity, they are settling for equality in oppression: they want men to be "sex objects" for them. The playgirl is pseudo-liberation from the playboy.

In this milieu of an impoverished ideal of human love and personal dignity and freedom, the choice of celibacy as a witness to the quality of human life in the Spirit of Christ makes sense to me. Of course that witness will be instructive and inspiring only if the celibacy in question includes, and is known to include, genuine human affection. If celibate life is presented or perceived as denial of human affection, withdrawal from interpersonal relationships, and negation of the body, emotions, and sexuality, then it will not succeed in teaching anybody about the quality of human life in the Spirit of Christ.

From the reflections of this chapter, we can conclude that the traditional reasons for celibacy do have validity as partial explanations of an individual's choice of celibacy. Celibacy does accomplish for individuals what the reasons claim for it. Those reasons can be partial motivation to opt for celibate life. We can also draw some conclusions about how the reasons for celibacy operate in any individual's choice.

First, not every reason for celibacy partially motivates any particular person's choice of celibacy. I am not aware of ever having been moved to choose celibacy in order to witness to resurrected life, where "they neither marry nor are given in marriage" (Matt. 11:30), or in order to witness to the union of the Church with her one spouse, Christ. As motives for celibacy, those reasons leave me unmoved. But someone else may be inspired by them in the context of their world-view and their value system.

Second, different reasons for celibacy are operative as motives with varying degrees of force at diverse times of life. Celibacy's provision of freedom for, and facilitation of, certain kinds of apostolic and pastoral activities has been a most constant partial motivation for my celibate life. The idea that Jesus recommended celibacy to his disciples moved me in some measure in early years of my life but not in later years. In times of questioning or struggle, the fact that Jesus lived a celibate life partially sustained me in my celibacy. As I became more appreciative of the supreme value of God's reign and of the beauty of life in the Spirit of Christ, and as I became more conscious of society's impoverished notions of love and sexuality, the more celibacy appealed to me as a means of giving witness to the transcendence of the kingdom and the quality of human life in Christ.

Worth noting in this consideration of changes in motivation is the fact that one may enter into celibate life for non-religious and even selfish motives, but acquire more appropriate religious, better-oriented motives later on. Perhaps by temperament, education, or unfortunate experience a person is not strongly attracted to marriage or intimacy of any sort. He or she finds a particular group of religious congenial to live and work with, or finds a ministry of hospital care, teaching, social work, or administration personally satisfying. For such motives the person enters a way of life of which celibacy is a part or assumes an office in the Church to which celibacy is annexed. It is possible, in fact very likely, that as life progresses and in one way or another his or her celibacy is challenged, questioned, informed by reflection on Scripture, or experienced as effective witness, the purely secular, self-centered motives will give way to authentic religious ones. This possibility or likelihood obviously supposes an openness to learning and being influenced. Wrong reasons for choosing celibate life can be replaced by correct reasons.

Third, the reasons for celibacy may be interpreted differently in the course of time. Once I thought celibacy was simply for the sake of the kingdom but now I think of it as for the sake of the kingdom to be realized through certain activities. Similarly I now understand celibacy's facilitation of apostolic and pastoral activity to concern certain kinds of activities, not all of which are the most important for the Church and world, and to refer more surely to the quantity of those activities than to their quality.

Fourth, a more important conclusion is that the reasons for celibacy assume their particular interpretations and their force in the context of concrete experiences and circumstances. Celibacy's power to liberate and to promote apostolic and pastoral activity functioned in my case as an ideal to be hoped for when I began celibate life. Today that power of celibacy functions motivationally as experienced fact; at the same time it receives a narrower interpretation than it had at the beginning of my celibate life. Jesus' own celibate life became a significant motivating factor in my own life mainly in times of questioning or struggle. In a context of growing faith in God, celibacy as witness to the transcendence of God's reign became an increasingly strong motive for my continuing choice of celibacy. Growing awareness of society's poor concept of love and sex provided the setting for choosing celibacy as a witness to the quality of life in Christ.

Finally, the reasons for celibacy function in the context of other motives for other activities, that is, in a larger value system shaping the whole of a person's life. If I had not desired to engage in certain apostolic and pastoral activities, I would not have sought the particular freedom celibacy provides or the particular aid it offers in carrying out those activities. Had I not sought growth in love of God and neighbor, celibacy as a means facilitating such growth would not have appealed to me. Only because of a prior wish for a full Christian life, for Christian perfection, did the presumed recommendation of celibacy attributed to Jesus move me to choose that style of life. Concern for God's reign and for the happiness of fellow human beings preceded the option for celibacy as witness to the transcendence of God's kingdom and the quality of human life in Christ.

These considerations reinforce the idea that celibacy is normally not chosen apart from choices of other values in life. It is not chosen as an end but as a means, not as a whole but as one part of a whole. It is one aspect of personal life among many other aspects; apart from these it makes no more sense than a single piece of a jigsaw puzzle. In vain does one seek to explain even partially one's own or another's choice of celibacy on the basis of one or several abstract reasons. These reasons appeal and move only as embodied in concrete lives rich in many respects—lives of celibate acquaintances or friends, lives of historical celibate figures, one's own celibate life projected imaginatively as a goal to be attained, or one's own celibate life actually experienced over a period of time. Celibacy is inextricably woven into the fabric of personal life and shares the mystery of that life.

From the reflections of this chapter I would draw practical advice for young people considering celibate life or already living it in virtue of a commitment to it for a few years in order to "try it out." The advice is not to dismiss too quickly the validity of the reasons offered for celibacy. In particular, they should not be dismissed because someone demonstrates that the same values can be found in Christian marriage. The fact that they are present in Christian marriage does not mean that they are absent from Christian celibate life. In each way of life they have an appropriate expression. Although every reason offered for celibacy is not valid for everyone, that is, does not move everyone who chooses celibate life, some people are moved by some reasons and other people by other reasons. They are so moved especially as celibate life is lived positively; then the reasons cease to be abstract notions and become experiences, part of that personal history which is God's call to celibate life—a call never totally illumined by a few "reasons" but always a mystery.

Chapter 3

A LIVING RESPONSE TO GOD

Religious celibacy, as we are understanding it here, is more than a choice of celibate life for religious reasons. It involves a promise or a vow to abide by that choice, even for a lifetime. But who can know himself or herself and his or her future well enough to make such a commitment? A pledge to a lifetime of celibacy, moreover, is a surrender of freedom. It is, therefore, incompatible with personal dignity and development. Not only does it close off other choices for other avenues of life, but it possibly condemns one to suffering and unhappiness. What answers are there for these common objections to any commitment to celibacy for life?

We can speak interchangeably of **promise** or **vow** or **pledge** of lifelong celibacy, or of **commitment** or **dedication** to such celibacy. Each expression has a different connotation but they all refer to the same act which is our concern here. Whatever name we give to this act, it is a religious act. It is directed to God the Father through his Son, Jesus Christ, in the power of the Holy Spirit. It is for the honor of the triune God. This religious aspect does not provoke the questions mentioned above, however; so our saying little about it here is not meant to deny or play down its importance. The act is problematic to people today because of the human component which is directed to God.

The human element in this act is not a declaration of accomplished fact. It is not an affirmation that one has actually lived celibately for the whole of one's life. Such a declaration is possible only on one's deathbed, for only then can one describe the whole of one's life and what one has actually done.

A vow of lifelong celibacy is not a prophecy or prediction that one will in fact live the whole of one's life as a celibate. No one knows the future well enough to make any such prophecy. We may conjecture what changes will occur in the world around us on the basis of what is going on there now, but history as well as our own experience remind us how fallible such conjectures are. Besides, we change over the years: our vision of life alters, our values shift, our response to surroundings differs. Though most of us do not change radically or totally over the years, we know from experience that we can change enough to make a once fulfilling situation no longer satisfying. A commitment to lifelong celibacy, then, is not to be understood as predicting future fact.

The promise or vow of celibacy for life is a declaration of intention made before God and the Church. It is setting a personal goal toward which one binds oneself to direct one's life as that life unfolds day by day. We do this sort of thing all the time. We decide upon a purchase to be made and hold ourselves to adjusting our daily spending to save money for it. We wish a holiday and make ourselves order each day's business so that we will have free time. Some people adopt a goal of marriage according to which they direct daily life, and some a goal of celibacy. If we did not intend goals and hold ourselves to pursuing them, we simply would not be living humanly.

After a declaration of intent to which we bind ourselves, some changes may come about in our circumstances which make it impossible or unwise for us to continue to order our lives toward that goal. It would be unreasonable to set an objective for ourselves in the first place if there were not some grounds for thinking that we could direct our lives toward it. Likewise it would be unreasonable to continue to guide our lives toward a goal if such changes occur that the goal becomes impossible of achievement, or if continued pursuit of it would be destructive to our physical, mental, or spiritual well-being. By granting dispensations from vows of celibacy, the Church recognizes that God does not hold us to the impossible or the destructive.

The idea of a vow of celibacy as a declaration of intention throws light on the knowledge of self and the future which is necessary for commitment to lifelong celibacy. One needs to know one's self now, in the present, and hence one's past which has made the self of the present. That knowledge takes account of one's needs, inclinations, interests, self-determination, self-control, and ability to endure privation. With such knowledge one must assess whether or not it is possible and wise to adopt lifetime celibacy as a goal. Are all the factors just mentioned so balanced that they are conducive to choosing celibate living day after day? If one's inclination for physical sexual intimacy is not balanced by an intense interest in apostolic or pastoral activity and an ability to endure the privation of physical sex, then it would be unreasonable to commit one's self to a life of celibacy. If one's desire for fatherhood or motherhood is not countered by a desire for service to a wide range of people and by a capacity to accept not being a father or a mother, to choose lifelong celibacy would be foolish.

We can never be absolutely certain of the correctness of our self-knowledge and our assessment of what the future can be. Our judgments will always have more or less probability. The choice of celibacy for life, as any other significant choice, entails risk and calls for trust

in God. If we did not make choices until we knew ourselves and our potential future perfectly and with certainty, we would never make any significant choices—for
celibacy, marriage, or anything else.

The choice of celibate life, the initial choice or the
choice to continue it, will always have attendant fears.
We can fear that life is passing us by, or that we may
learn too late whether we made the right choice for ourselves, or that we are dodging responsibility in not taking
a spouse and rearing children, or that our solitariness is
not a significant force for good after all. These fears and
others can induce us not to take the risk of choosing
celibacy. We need to learn to counter them with courage
in pursuit of what we believe is valuable, and with trust
in God that the evils these fears reflect will not be veri-
fied in the end. We need especially the support of other
celibates when the fears are more predominant.

As for the future, a promise of lifelong celibacy does
not require knowledge of what the future will have been,
as if such a promise were a statement of accomplished
fact. Nor does it require knowledge of what the future
will be, as if a pledge of lifelong celibacy were a prediction of future fact. It requires, rather, knowledge of
what we desire the future to be, for commitment is declaration of intention. Commitment to lifelong celibacy
creates the future which is intended.

We can face the future passively, letting it be determined by everyone and everything except ourselves.
The self which we will eventually be may be allowed to
emerge from acceptance of whatever experiences befall
us in the course of life. We can permit the ultimate shape
of our lives to be fixed by whatever circumstances we
pass through in time. Much of our lives is, of course,
given to us to accept, like breathing, feeling vigorous or
sluggish, imagining and thinking. Much is programmed
by forces external to us, like many of our patterns of

social interaction and our values. But much of our lives is also created by goals we set for ourselves and pursue. A chosen goal provides a focal point by which we evaluate and then accept or reject whatever opportunities come up as our lives unfold into the future. Toward this focal point we direct whatever experiences may occur. In view of this goal we pray for the helps which we need to achieve it—helps to be confidently expected from God who inspired the initial choice of the goal. Thus by means of commitment, whether of lifelong celibacy or lifelong marriage or some other objective, we fashion our lives in particular ways as we move into the future and meet whatever is there.

A promise of celibacy is not a surrender of freedom but its actualization. Freedom may be understood as the power to choose one of two or more alternative lines of action. Freedom in this sense is possibility (could be), not actuality (is). The person who never makes a choice lest he or she lose his or her freedom remains capable of doing many different deeds and of becoming many different persons, but he or she never actually does anything or becomes a particular person.

Some people drift through life without making any commitments, believing that they are remaining free, but they are remaining only potentially free. Their freedom stagnates at the level of **could be** and never reaches the level of **is.**

Actual freedom is a choice made while we could make another one. Actual freedom is achieved only when we give up a status of **could be** and choose **to be** in one way or another. In choosing a goal of lifelong celibacy, we actualize our freedom, become actually free and not merely potentially free. After the choice of lifetime celibacy, freedom does not cease. Potential freedom remains, and actual freedom is repeatedly called into existence in a multitude of choices in pursuit of the goal adopted.

To promise lifelong celibacy is to embark on a lifelong actualizing of our freedom, far removed from the surrender of freedom.

Rather than being incompatible with personal dignity, a pledge of celibacy for life and the subsequent choices that are made in fidelity to that pledge constitute personal dignity. Persons are distinctive in several ways. Persons are free beings, not totally determined in their behavior by instincts or circumstances. Of course, persons have bodies and psyches subject to the processes and rhythms of nature, but precisely as persons they transcend these natural functionings in some measure and determine the shape of their lives. A promise of lifetime celibacy and its consequent affirmations day by day are, as we have seen, actualizations of the freedom characteristic of persons. A pledge of lifelong celibacy generates personal dignity. It establishes personal dignity not only in a general, abstract way, that is, by exercising the freedom proper to persons. It constitutes a specific personal dignity; it makes one a particular kind of person, a celibate person.

Similarly, a vow to lifetime celibacy is not incompatible with personal development. Personal existence is a project, a creation; it entails taking one's life into one's own hands and shaping it according to one's own vision of what one wishes to be. Life as a project implies determining a goal and then ordering each moment's experience toward the attainment of that goal, thus developing one's personal being. If no goal is chosen, there is no possibility of shaping one's own life, but only of letting one's life be shaped by nature and circumstances. Rather than impeding personal development, dedication to a life of celibacy is one way of initiating such development.

The choice of celibacy for life does close off other avenues of life and other kinds of personal development.

This exclusion, however, is not the direct purpose of a pledge of celibate life but an inevitable, though not unique, by-product. In dedicating oneself to lifelong celibacy one actualizes freedom by the choice of a positive goal, a definite personal dignity, and a specific line of personal development. But it is part of the human condition that fulfillment, or actualization, or perfection, is achieved only by specification, or determination, and therefore by limitation. Paradoxically the perfection of a created being entails its limitation; its density of being involves narrowness of being. If we refrain from choice for fear of limiting ourselves, we doom ourselves to remaining imperfect, unfulfilled, and potentially free but not actually so. We limit ourselves even in choosing marriage and in selecting this partner rather than any other. Even not to choose marriage or celibacy is a limiting choice.

But does not a commitment to lifelong celibacy possibly condemn a person to unhappiness? After making a pledge of celibacy for life, someone may discover hitherto unrecognized personal needs or new values. The satisfaction of these needs may be incompatible with celibacy; or life according to these new values may conflict with celibate dedication. But the person is sentenced by his or her commitment to bear perpetual frustration of these needs or to live by values which have ceased to have meaning.

After vowing celibacy for life, not only may we discover personal needs or new values; we most probably will discover them, if we are alive. But the commitment to celibacy is creative of the future. As such it enables us to cope with what may arise as a cause of suffering; we are able to prevent that outcome and even promote personal development. For example, we may have chosen celibacy partially out of an understanding of self as having little need for other people. Afterwards we may learn from experience of a profound personal need for companionship generally and close relationships with one or a few people. We are not cut out for as much independence and solitude as youthful self-knowledge judged. Marriage may then appear to be the answer to the newly recognized need. But the vow of lifelong celibacy directs us to consider this need in the light of that chosen goal: What does the goal imply? What values does it have? And how does it contain an answer to the need? As a result of these considerations, we decide to meet the need by developing a more personal approach to God in prayer and a circle of friends, including a few very close ones.

These moves are not merely the satisfaction of a need but positive expressions of love of God and neighbor, for the sake of which celibacy was pledged initially. They constitute personal development. They actualize freedom and generate personal dignity. Rather than condemning to unhappiness when new needs or values are discovered, the commitment to lifelong celibacy is an instrument for handling these new factors in life in such a way as to promote personal fulfillment and greater love of God and neighbor.

Some privation may remain to cause a measure of suffering. There will be moments, in line with the example given, of great desire to share closely with someone and no one will be at hand; even God will seem distant, unhearing, silent. But the pain of these moments will not be so intense or lengthy as to render life as a whole unhappy. In fact, our spiritual resources may be able to turn even that unavoidable misery to good by gaining from it sensitivity to the suffering of the widowed, the elderly, the bedridden, the mentally disturbed, the outcasts of society. Perhaps if we never suffered loneliness precisely as a result of our vow of celibacy, we would never experience it in a way which would make us sensitive to other people's loneliness. Perhaps for us—we cannot speak of other people—this particular experience of loneliness is the way Providence chooses to make us compassionate servants. In any case, a promise of lifelong celibacy is not necessarily condemnation to unbearable suffering and unhappy life.

After vowing lifetime celibacy, if someone discovers needs and values whose claims are so great that he or she can no longer bear living celibately, the Church is willing to dispense from fulfillment of the vow. The Church may grant this dispensation only with other consequences, for example, no longer exercising the priesthood or no longer being a member of a religious congregation. But our concern here is with a commitment to celibacy as a possible source of suffering because of what celibacy itself directly excludes from life. Within this perspective, the Church's willingness to dispense guarantees that the vow need not be condemnation to unhappiness from the specific denials inherent in lifelong celibacy. Some celibates may cling to their misery in celibate life because of social pressure, fear of shame, lack of courage, guilt feelings about abandoning a course of life once chosen but now seen as impossible or unwise, or unwillingness to give up a ministry or living conditions associated with celibacy. If such is the case, then the unhappiness resulting from continuing in celibate life should be attributed to these causes and not to the promise of lifelong celibacy.

So far in this chapter we have been thinking about celibacy in terms of something we do individually: I promise, vow, pledge celibacy for life; I commit or dedicate myself to it; then I proceed to carry out my proposal. The image here is of a man or woman weighing the future, mustering his or her resources, building up boldness in view of the uncertainties of the future, daringly making a decision, and henceforth clinging to that decision whatever happens. Celibacy appears to be a stance once assumed and then stubbornly maintained throughout life. It seems to be a rigid framework in which life is lived, not life itself. It is personal but not interpersonal.

The language of **commitment, vow, carrying out a promise, fidelity to one's pledge** is certainly applicable to lifelong celibacy, but it does not do justice to celibate life. As we have seen in chapter one, celibacy is a gift before it is a commitment and the fulfillment of that commitment. Celibacy issues from multiple factors influencing one's personal history, culminating in a desire or at least a willingness to promise celibacy and live it. In faith we see this personal history as an enabling invitation from God. A commitment to celibacy and fulfillment of that pledge are, therefore, responses to God inviting a person to a way of life that, in its distinctive way, is for him, that is, for God.

Thus celibacy is not merely personal, that is, a person's free decision determining his or her personal dignity. The decision to live celibately ultimately does not arise solely out of a person's own resources; and fidelity to that decision is not simply faithfulness to one's self. Celibacy is also and importantly interpersonal, a person's response to a personal God, that is, a God who knows and cares about him or her. It is a response, moreover, issuing from God's invitation inherent in one's personal history enabling the response.

The response to God which is celibacy is not a once-for-all act but a daily one, sometimes even an hourly one. There is the initial reply when one first begins to think about a commitment to celibacy because one perceives a thrust or openness in oneself toward that way of life. If self-knowledge confirms that inclination as an invitation from God, acceptance of self so inclined is a further response to God and the actual promise of lifelong celibacy another answer. A commitment to celibacy becomes part of one's history; it becomes a factor in that past which constitutes the person of the present and points to his or her future; it becomes one of those many influences over a lifetime which coalesce to constitute God's call to an individual to a particular personality development, career, and way of life. Fidelity to a vow is not merely faithfulness to one's own prior act, to one's own self. It is more significantly response to God's invitation which has now assumed the form, not only of a given inclination, but also the form of a freely chosen and declared intention to which one has bound self. Fidelity to a vow is fidelity to God calling one through that pledge.

Challenges to celibate living evoke new understandings of celibacy and repeated confirmations of the promise of celibacy; these new understandings and confirmations are additional replies to God. Challenges also prompt prayer for God's assistance in persevering in one's celibate commitment. That prayer becomes part of one's personal history, a sign of God's call, and at the same time a fashioning of one's future in response to God's call. To God one has pledged celibacy for the sake of his reign, and his response can be counted on. Thus celibate life is continuing response to God, indeed dialogue with him, a dynamic communion.

Celibate life conceived as ongoing faithful response to God inviting us to live by, with, and for him opens the way to a conception of celibate life as changing and growing. In the course of a lifetime, God's invitation appears in a variety of circumstances; the mysterious inner thrust or openness to celibate life is felt in a variety of situations. It must be discerned and responded to in a variety of ways. Each set of circumstances evokes distinct and new insights into what God's invitation is, and each set calls for an appropriate celibate response. For

example, the invitation to celibacy may appear initially
to a young person as a call chiefly to forego the satisfactions and fulfillments of sexuality with regard to its
physical aspects, be this sensual pleasure or becoming
father or mother. At this stage of life a celibate response
to God may be discerned as mainly a matter of discipline
over bodily cravings and urges which at times are very
intense and absorb attention which should be given to
God and neighbor.

Later in life, when one is engaged in ministry and
responsible and concerned about others to a greater extent, the invitation to celibacy may appear much more
as a call to share one's time and energy and person with
an ever wider circle of people, a call to be deeply involved in the welfare of a family not of three, six, or ten
people but of dozens, hundreds, a whole parish. Foregoing physical sexuality and parenthood appears a necessary but secondary element of celibacy, as does the
exercise of self-control of bodily urges and emotional
longings. One responds to God's call in a spirit of generous giving of self in the service of as many people as
possible.

At still another stage of life, when the joys of serving
others become familiar, the limitations of human efforts
more apparent, and the passage of people through one's
life an accepted fact, the call to celibacy appears in life's
commonplaceness, imperfection, loneliness. The call is
discerned as an invitation to draw more closely to God,
the Fullness of Being and the Source of ultimate satisfaction. The response is more intense, perhaps more
lengthy, prayer. Strong attraction to a person of the
opposite sex and growth of friendship may occasion still
another hearing of God's invitation to celibacy, discern-
ment of new dimensions of it, and a new way of living it.
Celibacy is thus not a straitjacket confining life but a
living response to God who calls continually in a variety

of unpredictable manners, so that celibate life alters and grows as God's call is variously perceived.

At this point we can take up a question which has generated much debate in recent years. What are we to think about those who depart from religious life or the priesthood after promising lifelong celibacy? Are we to say that they have been unfaithful to their commitments and above all to God? To make that claim appears to be the logical conclusion of the idea of vocation we have been developing here. If vocation is embedded in one's personal history, if one's promise to live celibately for life is part of that history, and, as is often the case, if that history includes having lived celibately for a period of time, then to depart from celibate life is forsaking one's vocation. If it is argued that one's personality and circumstances may have changed after the promise of lifelong celibacy so that one's personal history now contains a new call from God for a new way of life, it may be asked how this change came about. If it occurred by deliberate choice, by willful neglect, or by conscious indifference, then the point of infidelity to God and to one's own pledge is simply relocated prior to the actual decision to leave.

The question may be put in more objective terms. Is there such a thing as a temporary vocation to vowed celibate life? Attempts to answer this question can become ensnarled in the meaning of **vocation,** that is, whether or not the word should be reserved to ways of life which society or the Church regard as permanent. But supposing that it can be used of non-permanent ways of life, is it possible to have a temporary vocation when one has promised to live celibately for a lifetime?

In the past several years many brothers, sisters, and priests have departed from religious life and the clerical state after long struggle, much anguish, and many tears. The majority of them have been earnest, sincere people.

To brand them all as having betrayed their commitments and having turned their backs on God is absurd as well as unchristian. Some had only temporal vows, that is, commitments to celibacy for a year or three years, and merely let those vows lapse, as they had a right to do. Others did have pledges of lifelong celibacy. How can we interpret their setting aside celibacy after promising to live it for life in response to God's call?

We might invoke the customary theory about dispensation from vows. A vowed celibate, after careful consideration, may decide that so much has changed in his or her personality or circumstances that celibate life is now impossible or extremely difficult; it entails so great a struggle that it generates paralyzing unhappiness; for this person it is no longer a "better good," the quality required traditionally for the object of a vow. The celibate may then ask the Church to dispense from fulfilling the pledge. The Church, in dispensing, confirms the celibate's judgment about the situation and frees him or her from the obligation of keeping the promise. But the vow, promise, pledge remains; the celibate cannot undo the past historical fact, nor can the Church. The pledge remains to become obliging again if and when circumstances become favorable for its fulfillment. The latter, however, rarely happens in the case of celibacy, for one may marry or, even if one does not marry, other changes take place in one's life which justify continuing dispensation.

Thus religious and priests asking for and receiving dispensation by the Church from living celibate life are not betraying their commitment or rejecting God's call. The commitment and call remain. Only the response to the call and the fulfillment of the commitment are set aside as a result of an honest judgment, confirmed by the Church, that they no longer constitute a "better good" for the person involved.

This answer explains the Church's role in dispensing from vows. It also expresses the respect which the Church has for the mystery of an individual's encounter with God in a promise or pledge to him. The Church refrains from claiming any power over that intimate religious experience either on the person's side or God's side. The Church limits itself to a judgment about the feasibility of carrying out now what was initiated in that mysterious, sacred encounter in the past. In so acting the Church is counselling and confirming the individual in his or her decision and also providing for public order in the Church.

But this answer is not satisfactory in accounting for many individuals' experience in leaving religious life or priestly celibacy. First of all, this answer implies failure on the part of the celibate. The failure is not necessarily moral, but it is at least a failure in the sense of inability, physical or psychological, to triumph over obstacles. The dispensation is given precisely on the grounds that personal development or changing environment have so altered one's situation that one can no longer manage to live celibately without distress and unhappiness. To consider everyone seeking dispensation from vowed celibacy as failing, morally or in some other way, presumes a rather dismal view of the quality of the men and women who have been and are in religious life and the priesthood. It is also unkind to those who leave; it adds to their struggle to build a new life the burden of overcoming a stigma of failure. Above all, it does not reflect the experience of self-discovery, freedom, achievement, and peace which these people have. For them, setting aside religious celibacy is not a negative experience, but a positive one—discovering new life for God and neighbor.

This answer also puts in question the value of the rest of the dispensed person's life. Suppose that the person marries. Can he or she derive joy in good times and strength in bad times from the thought that his or her marriage is God's gift and that the effort to make it work is his or her response to God's graciousness? The answer is a qualified "Yes but. . . ." The authentic call, gift, and response are to another way of life than this marriage, and they would revive if one only had the required fiber of being to overcome obstacles. This marriage is a God-given vocation, but a substitute for the real one, necessitated by inability to respond to the first one. Or this marriage is a God-given vocation objectively speaking: God is the author of marriage; but it is not a God-given vocation subjectively speaking: God has not positively called this person to marriage but only permitted him or her to enter marriage because of inability to accept his or her authentic vocation to celibate life.

This trend of thought is repugnant to human nature; a person who leaves celibate life would have to fight against it at the risk of otherwise becoming depressed and impaired for living. It also clashes with an idea of the human person as freely constituting himself or herself as a person. It does not tally with a concept of God as willing men's and women's total betterment.

Another interpretation may be offered for abandonment of a lifetime commitment to celibacy. This interpretation sees an analogy with annulments now granted more readily by the Church in marriage cases. Today it is recognized that someone may not have the personal psychological resources to fulfill the responsibilities of marriage in general or of marriage to a particular person, even as someone may be physically impotent generally or in relation to a particular person. Moreover, a valid marriage covenant requires of the parties not only their rational knowledge of the objective nature of marriage and its responsibilities, but also adequate knowledge of their subjective psychological capacity to fulfill the obligations of this marriage. One cannot promise to give what one lacks the capacity to give. Adequate knowledge of subjective resources is not always achieved early in life, or easily achieved, or readily ascertainable by others. In fact, the absence of subjective capacity frequently comes to light only after a marriage is under way, perhaps even long into a marriage, at a time of crisis or in a period of stress. From the beginning there was no vocation to this marriage, and the covenant to it was null from the outset, but all this is recognized only belatedly.

In religious life and the priesthood also it is possible for someone to make a commitment for which the psychological capacity to fulfill it is wanting, but knowledge of this want is lacking at the time the promise is made. If someone does not have the psychological capacity to live celibately for a lifetime, he or she cannot promise to live that way, since it is impossible for him or her. But this inability may be recognized only after a vow was made and even lived for sometime in good faith. When the psychological inability is finally recognized, a dispensation from the vow is perfectly in order.

This interpretation does not involve the notion of failure and it explains the sense of self-discovery, the relief, and the contentment which many priests and religious experience as part of a decision to leave religious life or the celibate priesthood. But the interpretation still entails an idea of inadequacy, which may not be much less debilitating or any more easy to overcome than a concept of failure. It also does not explain positively the religious value of the commitment that was made and of all the years spent living celibately. If we examine a common case, perhaps we can state a similar but more satisfying interpretation.

A young woman entered religious life after high school. She was attracted to this way of life, including celibacy, to some degree and for a variety of reasons, some healthy, some perhaps not so sound, but her desire to become a religious was basically as valid as most people's choices for one career or another. After entrance she lived in a milieu which shielded her from experiences that would make another way of life attractive and religious life unattractive. She was educated in ways which supported and reinforced her ability to be content and even comfortable in religious and celibate life. Questions whether this life was really meant for her came up periodically, sometimes forcefully, sometimes vaguely. She put the questions aside, occasionally with a satisfying answer, at other times with no answer at all. She had a normal measure of success in sublimating her instinctual drive for mating and motherhood by devotion to Christ, care for her companions in religious life, and service of people. She strove to be a good religious living for God, and she was. When the time came for perpetual vows, she made them in the belief that she was called by God to this way of life.

Some years later she moved into a situation of life and work quite different from what she had previously experienced in religious life. As a result of new personal experiences, she grew in self-knowledge. She discerned new values, some long held but unrecognized, some never before seen, all of which relativized the values by which she had been living. Questions about her way of life began to receive different answers. She eventually concluded that religious life was not her radical vocation from God, but only the vocation that she had perceived. So she chose to leave religious life and follow her radical vocation.

In this case, the woman's choice of another way of life issued from greater experience of life and greater self-knowledge; it followed from personal growth, not failure. On the other hand, her years of religious life were not a mistake, an error. She chose that life on the basis of a prudential judgment that God was calling her. Prudential judgments about how to act and live concretely have, at most, moral certitude. If one word must be used for this kind of certitude, it would be called "probability" rather than "certainty." Such judgments, moreover, are subject to being changed under new circumstances; their being changed does not mean they were wrong, for their truth depends on their appropriateness to the circumstances in which they are made. On the basis of such a judgment, this woman lived a genuine religious life in response to God whom she perceived as calling her. If God's call is embedded in personal history, he was indeed calling her in her prudential judgment which sprung from her past and interpreted that past as a divine call to religious life.

In this case we have distinguished between a radical vocation and a perceived vocation. The perceived vocation was a real vocation and the foundation for an authentic religious life. It was dependent, however, upon a certain range of experience and a certain level of self-knowledge. The commitment to perpetual celibacy was proportioned to that vocation and its conditions, although the language used in profession did not reveal this qualification which is presumed in prudential judgments. When personal experience had broadened, when a new level of self-knowledge was achieved, when the radical vocation was discerned in personal history, when the conditional quality of the vocation to religious life and of the promise of perpetual celibacy became apparent—when all these events occurred, the perceived vocation was set aside for the radical one. This move can hardly be called a rejection of God's call and a betrayal of commitment. It was, on the contrary, a response to God's call now more accurately discerned in personal history, and a recognition of the conditioned character of the commitment.

The crucial moment in this case is the time in which

this woman found herself in new circumstances involving fresh personal experiences leading to further self-knowledge, different values, and novel answers to her questions about her vocation. In this period she could be said, under certain conditions, to have failed or even to have betrayed her commitment and rejected God's call. This judgment could be made if she entered into the new situation and reacted to what happened there without caring about where she would be led. If she had no reasons for greater self-knowledge, new values, and different answers to her vocation questions, or if she neglected to protect and develop what she believed to be her vocation, an adverse judgment could be made against her. In the case under consideration, however, none of these conditions existed. None of them have existed in the cases of many other priests and religious who have departed after promising perpetual celibacy.

The Church, the People of God as well as its apostolic office, regards perpetual vows or promises as signs of radical vocation and as introductions into a permanent style of life. But we have to distinguish public order from private life. The Church in dispensing from vows is making this distinction. It admits that within and beneath the order it sets up for ordinary public ecclesial life are mysterious encounters of its individual members with God; these encounters do not always tally perfectly with their place in the public order. The same may be said for the Church's regarding the priesthood as a lifetime office and yet laicizing men who decide that their vocation is not to that office as it is concretely realized in the Church. The Church in granting release from religious life or the priesthood, and specifically from celibate life, is not declaring that the departing religious or priest has failed or has betrayed his or her commitment, but only that his or her individual relationship to God has developed in a direction which no longer corresponds to the place in the public order of the Church which he or she has occupied.

What about a person who leaves religious life or the priesthood and then returns? It may happen that someone is dispensed from her or his celibate commitment and pursues another style of life. Then she or he discovers that what was judged to be her or his radical vocation really is not; it too is only a perceived vocation. The lifetime celibacy originally adopted and then conscientiously set aside is, after all, the radical calling. Some individuals may find their radical vocation only after such experience. We should not be surprised that the discovery of vocation follows this course if God's call assumes the form of personal history and comes to light in self-knowledge and to realization in self-acceptance. For some people to discover and accept their radical identity and vocation may take longer than for others.

The interpretation offered here for departure from religious life or the priesthood and specifically from lifelong celibacy remains in the framework of familiar ideas of God's providence and man's role under providence. According to these conceptions, a person's vocation is fixed by God and a person's task is to discover and conform to what God has determined. Another interpretation could be developed on the basis of contemporary theology. In this view one's personal, freely-shaped life develops, not according to some predetermined divine plan, but in a dialogue between the divine Persons and the created person. A person's radical vocation is not something already made by God to be discovered, but something to be made in cooperation with God. In either interpretation, it is possible to see in departure from religious life or the priesthood, and specifically from lifelong celibacy, not failure or betrayal and rejection, but personal growth, achievement, and a source of peace.

Yet I must confess that in some cases it is difficult for

me not to wonder if there has not been failure or betrayal—not gross failure or vicious betrayal, but some
neglect of prayer, some withdrawal from one's own community of religious or priests, some over-reliance on one's
own activity, some excessive absorption in ministry,
some assumption of purely secular values, some forgetfulness of the ideals of religious or priestly celibacy.
The failure or betrayal may often be equally or even
chiefly that of the religious community or diocesan presbyterium who did not keep their side of the bargain to
support and to stimulate to continual growth the woman
or man whom they once so eagerly welcomed into their
midst.

We would be unwise to forget the human condition
in which failure and betrayal unfortunately can and do
occur. We would be unwise, not because our business
is to judge others, but because we wish to do what is
necessary for ourselves in order to be faithful in our own
loving response to God, and we wish to give our brothers
and sisters the support they need to be faithful in their
response. The human condition should prompt us especially to pray for the faithful choice of celibate life for
ourselves and our brothers and sisters, because it is, as
we noted earlier, a gift from God before it is our choice
or commitment.

In his encyclical **On the Celibacy of Priests** (24 June
1967), Pope Paul VI expressed a conviction of faith,
namely, that a choice for celibacy made with human and
Christian prudence is a choice given by a grace which
does not destroy but perfects nature; that the Creator
and Redeemer knows what he can ask of us and gives
us everything we need to do what he asks; and that the
grace and fidelity humbly and perseveringly prayed for
will never be denied (nos. 51, 74). Such a conviction ren-
ders more mysterious—to me at least—the course which
the lives of some sincere celibates have taken. When re-

moved from the abstract and mingled with the complexities of an individual's life, its clarity may be obscured and its power to sustain hampered. Nevertheless, it is a conviction of faith to be fostered and helps us to accept difficulties in living celibately as part of the adventure of celibacy.

Chapter 4

AN ADVENTURE IN LIVING

The word adventure connotes a positive undertaking, like discovering the source of the Nile River or scaling Mount Everest. It involves struggling to meet challenges: limited human energies, diseases, difficult or dangerous terrain, extremes of heat or cold. In meeting challenges there are advances and reverses, successes and failures. Adventure entails planning ingeniously, mustering courage, attempting, failing, revising strategy, renewing courage, trying again, and persevering through challenge after challenge until the goal is reached. The outcome of adventure is uncertain: challenges to progress along the way may not be overcome; the final attempt at the goal may fail. Adventure means taking risks and requires daring, courage, patience, and perseverance. It means achievement, at least the very struggle with opposing forces, but also completion of part of the journey and eventually attaining the goal. Adventure is stimulating and exciting; it gives zest to life and a feeling of satisfaction.

Religious celibacy is an adventure in living humanly. This affirmation may surprise those who see celibacy only or mainly in terms of what is foregone in celibate life—the many-faceted fulfillment of marriage and family. But celibate life has all the characteristics of adventure, not merely an adventure inserted into life but an adventure whose enterprise is life itself. Married life deserves to be called an adventure, but so does celibate life.

To appreciate this view of celibacy, it is necessary first of all to see celibacy primarily as a positive thrust of life, an impulse for something. The thrust or impulse may be very strong and undeniable, or subtle and questionable, or alternately both. It is diffuse, complex, and mysterious, but it is there. Without it there is no undertaking of celibate life or continuing in it, though undoubtedly some people "go through the motions" of celibate life, as some people go through the motions of marriage. Celibacy does entail self-denial, but because it is first of all self-transcendence; something is left behind in the process of going beyond it toward some goal. Celibacy may indeed be sublimation, but sublimation gives direction to psychic energy, and this energy is a positive force. Celibacy is not not-doing but doing.

What is done in being celibate varies from person to person. It may vary even in the mind of the same person from time to time. Sometimes that which is being done may be obscure, confused, or dubious; and then the celibate will be troubled about his or her life. But over the course of time the celibate is living for something; his or her celibate life is a positive enterprise.

I can recall one moment in my life in which the desire for celibate life was particularly vigorous and vivid. It occurred in my nineteenth year, not long after entering the major seminary. I was in the periodical section of the library. Undoubtedly I was reading but more certainly my thoughts were ranging far from what I was reading. I was feeling intensely happy with my life, my vocation to the priesthood, the beginning of advanced studies for the priesthood, my friends, and the experiences which I shared with them. In all this I saw God's goodness to me and a beauty of life which Christianity made possible. I felt a tremendous desire to share that happiness and that Christianity with as many other people as possible. Celibacy was included explicitly in that desire as a means to the end. Basically my celibacy was a desire to share with many the good which I felt God had given me.

No doubt a psychiatrist could delight in analyzing that experience! But I simply could not believe him if he were to tell me that I became or am celibate fundamentally because I fear sex or love or intimacy or responsibility. I do not claim to be free of all such fears. I am sure I have my share of them. I would not be surprised to learn that they have influenced my initial choice of celibacy and its continuation. But I am certain that my celibacy is not primarily or principally a running away or a giving up, but a pursuit. That experience of many years ago and other experiences, less vivid and memorable and involving different motives, assure me that my celibacy is not withdrawal from life but a positive project of life.

Many people find it difficult to understand the positive thrust in celibacy. No doubt it is not fully understandable to those who have not experienced it, who stand outside rather than inside celibate experience. But the fact is that men and women can be and are so caught up by the desire for God or by the Christian vision for humanity or by the plight of the needy that they are not so intensely interested in the satisfactions of genital sexuality or the intimate living of marriage or raising children. Yes, they feel the urge for genital pleasure, the hunger for intimacy, the longing for children of their own, but another yearning impels them to forego the fulfillment of those desires for another purpose.

This yearning which is the core of celibacy can be illusory, of course. One's desire for God, the reign of Christ, or the relief of the poor may bear upon romantic fantasy rather than hard reality. Celibacy based on illusion is a mistake leading to no good. Similarly, if the positive thrust of celibacy is to be healthily human, it must be tempered to respect personal needs for companionship, friends, rest, recreation, and similar basics recognized even by the most austere monks of old. It must also be measured by a realistic assessment of how much the celibate can do for others. Much of the time he or she will be touching only the outer layers of people's lives. When he or she does embrace the whole of others' lives or enter into secret chambers, it will usually be for a short time only. The thrust of celibacy must also correspond to the realities of religious or priestly life, such as periods of aridity in prayer, conflicting goals among associates in community or ministry, the dulling effect of routine, the subtle fact that community does not happen, nor is it made once for all, but is always in the making.

To rule out illusion as the basis of celibacy's thrust is not to rule out idealism. The hopes and expectations of young men and women leaning toward, or entering upon, celibate life will very likely be idealistic, not taking into account some of the facts of life which will try their mettle. But idealism is healthy at this age, the fuel of magnanimous life-projects. Older celibates can be grateful for the renewed inspiration such idealism affords. In a balanced personality, experience will temper this idealism, not destroying it but concretizing it in realizable forms. The models for realizable celibate life are older celibates who are happy, sensitive, and productive men and women.

A frequent perilous illusion envisions celibacy as an instituted way of life which will automatically yield fulfillment and happiness. The twin of this illusion presents the institution of marriage as an alternate guaranteed route to happiness and satisfaction. When celibate life becomes difficult, the inclination is to suspect that the wrong state of life has been chosen and that marriage should be embraced instead.

Undoubtedly a person's fulfillment and happiness can be seriously affected by the institutional situation in which he or she lives. But it is an illusion to think that one or another institution guarantees happiness. Neither the state of marriage nor that of celibacy substitutes for personal responsibility to make one's own life. No other person and much less any institution can make human beings out of us. They can help us; we can profit from them; but the responsibility for our lives and the creation of satisfying lives is ours. To blame another person or an institution for our misery accomplishes nothing but more misery. It is refusal to bear responsibility. To abandon one institution for another in that frame of mind solves nothing.

Celibacy, then, like adventure, is a positive undertaking. Also like adventure, it implies struggles to meet challenges. Attainment of the goal toward which celibacy is a positive thrust may be frustrated. One's celibacy may be in its core an all-absorbing desire for profound communion with God, but God remains hidden. Prayer proves an arid experience. Or much effort is invested in it with meager yield compared to expectations. Bringing the message and love of Christ to many others may be the longing underlying one's celibacy, but the others remain indifferent or refuse or become hostile. If they are receptive, they may not express any gratitude. Most of them, moreover, pass out of the celibate's life in a relatively short time.

Thus the celibate is challenged to deal with feelings of failure, disappointment, dissatisfaction, lack of fulfillment. While struggles with such feelings are not unique to celibates, they do have to handle them without the help of a loving and understanding spouse. Others—widows, single people, sometimes even the married—are, of course, in the same situation. But that fact does not lessen the poignancy of the celibate's own feelings or the aloneness in which he or she struggles, though it may prevent excessive self-pity if recognized.

In celibacy's thrust toward its goal, the usual satisfaction of certain human needs are by-passed. The celibate foregoes deliberately willed genital sexual pleasure and a range of sensuous pleasures insofar as they may lead to genital pleasure. Though the celibate does not deliberately will these pleasures, the body-self never completely ceases to cry out for them. Moreover, willynilly, they are felt more or less frequently with greater or lesser intensity. The body's hunger for them or the allure of their presence can be at times almost overpowering or actually so. The celibate has to struggle to discipline himself or herself to control, or at least pay no attention to, the urges or the pleasures which he or she feels welling up from within, lest he or she not abstain from genital sex but abuse it.

The celibate must strive also to moderate the control which he or she seeks over genital sex. If the control is excessive, the celibate suppresses not only the pleasures of genital sex but also sensuous pleasures remotely but not necessarily connected to genital sex, and other kinds of pleasure too. This range of pleasures may be legitimate and even necessary for mental health, human dignity, and the sensitivity necessary to serve God and others well. There are such things as modest kisses and embraces; celibacy does not exclude them. One remedy for sorrow, according to St. Thomas (**Summa theologiae,** I-II, q. 38, a. 5), is sleep and a hot bath. Celibacy is not meant to negate bodily life but to direct it.

Struggle in regard to genital sex is, of course, not unique to celibate life. The single person desirous of practicing Christian chastity has a similar struggle. Even the married are challenged to achieve wholesome genital sex. In the early phase of marriage a common problem is "sexual adjustment" between the partners. Throughout married life the problem occasionally arises when one partner feels a great need for sexual satisfaction while the other does not.

The drive for genital sex is one of the most powerful forces of nature with which human beings must deal. Marriage is not simply passive surrender to it, for it can be demonic and destructive as well as playful and enriching. Marriage, like celibacy, is a way of handling nature's drive in a manner appropriate to human dignity. Celibacy does not differ from marriage because celibacy entails a challenge to humanize genital sex and marriage does not. Both pursue humanizing genital sex but in different ways. Both involve struggle, but a different one.

Some people regard the celibate's challenge to forego genital sexuality as the supreme struggle of celibacy. How can anyone renounce the pleasure of sexual foreplay and orgasm which throughout human history have been judged the most exquisitely satisfying physical pleasure man or woman can have? How can anyone resist the frequent vehement urges for such pleasures?

The fact is that people can and do discipline themselves to withstand those inclinations and live without the pleasure toward which they tend. With practice, it becomes easier not to surrender to desires and to live without the gratification of genital sex.

This ability can be gained, moreover, without adverse effects on personality. Living celibately is not merely a matter of fighting countless battles against insurgent physical urges or enduring privation of something whose lure is unceasingly before the eyes of the mind. Resistance becomes an art, an ability to divert attention from what arouses feelings and to sublimate energies to other outlets. Foregoing genital satisfaction becomes simply the negative side of absorbing interest in other values. In time, the urge for genital pleasure is either less vehement, or more readily prevented in the first place, or more easily counteracted when aroused. The absence of genital gratification is missed less and less, compensated for by other satisfactions. Celibacy is not frustration of bodily desires but discipline and sublimation; it is human; it is virtue, which Paul Tillich translates from the Greek word **arete** (in Latin **virtus**) as "humanity," in the sense of the full realization of human potential.[1]

If a celibate regularly over a long period has difficulty resisting the enjoyment of physical sex, this is most likely due to some other problem with which he or she is struggling. Frustration may be occurring in efforts to achieve goals for which celibacy was chosen in the first place. The positive thrust which is the core of celibacy has weakened or broken down for some reason. More general sexual needs, like occasional companionship or work with someone of the opposite sex, or basic human needs, like those for recognition, respect, love, achievement, are not being fulfilled. In such cases the celibate's indulgence in genital pleasure is a symptom of a deeper problem than inability to control the impulse for physical sex.

Greater by far than celibacy's challenges on the physical plane are those on the psychological. Loneliness is not unique to the celibate. The widowed know it, as do married people separated for a time from their spouses and families. Indeed, the experience can be more painful for them than for celibates who are not accustomed to the close companionship of spouse and children. But the

---

1—*Systematic Theology*, III (Chicago: University of Chicago Press, 1963), p. 67.

celibate is frequently reminded that he or she is alone. From the travel section of the Sunday newspapers, it becomes obvious that vacations are for two. The people whom the celibate meets at social events are, for the most part, couples. When the celibate sees another man or woman with his or her spouse, the celibate is sometimes painfully reminded that he or she could have such an attractive companion as an intimate part of his or her life. For the celibate who does not live in community, and even for some who do, it can be a desolate experience to see the last family leave the Church grounds after the bustle of Sunday morning Masses and then to walk alone to a silent rectory. It would not be more satisfying to go into some of the homes of the families who have just been at Mass, and it may even be painful; family life is not all light and sweetness. But still there is the thought of, and hunger for, the warmth and companionship of spouse and children.

This need for companionship is also a need for the companionship of the opposite sex. In relating to someone of the opposite sex, different complexes of emotions and behavior are called into action which are not active when dealing with the same sex. This fact may be cultural in its origin, but it is nonetheless real and very likely will be the case for a long time to come. If not for survival, then at least for a well-rounded personality, the company of the opposite sex is a need.

The celibate longs for more than companionship. He or she longs to be loved and to love, indeed to be special to someone and to hold another as special. The need to be loved, to be accepted, prized, treasured for ourselves, not just for our work or wit or talents, begins with our existence and persists to the end. Without being loved, we die, perhaps literally, as happened in England during World War II to babies taken from their families into safer shelters in the countryside where, however, they did not receive sufficient personal, loving care. We want to love as well as be loved, for loving lifts us out of ourselves, expands our world, enriches us with more life, namely, the lives of those whom we love, who become other selves in our love for them.

We yearn for still more: we desire to be special to someone and to cherish someone as special to us. What all the sources of this desire are, I do not know; but we see it functioning all around us. Perhaps we need to be special to someone for the final confirmation of our selves, the final "You're O.K." Perhaps we need to cherish someone as special because we need to love but are finite in our capacity to think about, care for, and give to others. We can fully satisfy our need to cherish only by focusing on one person, even though we love many more people than only this one.

The inclination toward a special love in our lives is probably related to another need, namely, for intimacy. By **intimacy** I mean the mutual sharing of inner selves. There is, of course, sensuous and sexual intimacy, the mutual sharing of bodily selves. But that is not the kind of intimacy meant here. We are talking about sharing the thoughts that run through our minds, the fears and desires which influence our decisions, the aspirations which inspire us, the reactions we feel to specific persons, situations, and events—especially those thoughts, emotions, reactions which we do not express in our ordinary daily commerce with other people.

We need such intimacy in our lives. We need to express our inner selves simply to have an inner life. By nature, some philosophers tell us, we have experience precisely by the symbolic transformation of reality, by giving expression to our being and our interaction with persons and the world. Even the silent person, whom we might be inclined to say does not express himself or herself, is expressing as a matter of fact, by his or her taciturnity, that something is going on within. The sign is obscure and ambiguous: it may manifest thoughtfulness or it may signal paralyzing fear of a situation, perhaps subconscious fear. But the silence is definitely an expression of inner life.

We need to express our inner selves also to clarify for ourselves what is going on there, so that we can assimilate it into our lives or reject it. If we keep everything to ourselves, the whole of it becomes confused and confusing and impairs realistic, peaceful living. By expressing our inner selves we can also release pressures of anxiety, guilt, and shame. Feedback from others, helpful for dealing with our problems, can come to us only if we attempt to manifest what is on our minds. Support from others in our inner life, whether in our most cherished ambition or in our most painful hurt, presupposes that we reveal this life to others. Intimacy with different people and in varying degrees is normally necessary for healthy human life.

Another psychological need, connected with our biological nature, is for parenthood. Most men and women desire, in varying degrees, to generate new life, not merely biological life but human life. Nature seeks to perpetuate itself through our persons, and we feel not only nature's physical push toward mating but also psychological urges to father and to mother others. In fact, these impulses sometimes get out of control and impede the very life they seek to promote, as when parents dominate their children and refuse to let them grow up. In Erik Erikson's scheme of personality development through eight stages, the sixth stage is a struggle to achieve intimacy rather than isolation, and the seventh stage calls for an effort at generativity in preference to stagnation.[2] This generativity is more than the mere fact of wanting or having children; it is a broader concern for establishing and guiding the next generation, either one's own offspring or others'. Generativity is necessary for maturity, for the mature person needs to be needed, and maturity requires guidance and encouragement from what it has produced and must care for.

In foregoing marriage, the celibate sets aside a context of life which offers rich opportunities, indeed unique opportunities, for the fulfillment of these psychological needs. Marriage, of course, does not automatically satisfy them. Married people must struggle with the fears which surround these needs or the attempts to fulfill them. The temptations to satisfy these needs in selfish or perverse ways must be grappled with even in marriage. But marriage does offer unique opportunities for companionship, relating to the opposite sex, loving and being loved, cherishing and being cherished, intimacy, and fathering and mothering.

Throughout his or her life, the celibate occasionally feels twinges of longing at the sight of a married couple or a father or mother with a child. There are moments of profound loneliness, of longing to be hugged, of yearning to share inner life with someone who deeply cares about it. That such desires and consciousness of want arise, however, is not a sign that the wrong style of life has been chosen. On the contrary, such feelings and awareness are signs that the celibate is a healthy human being, and that the life offered to God is indeed a precious gift to him. They are signs too that the celibate is capable of being a compassionate servant of God's people. They are also a challenge to the celibate to satisfy these deep

---

2—*Childhood and Society* (2nd ed.; New York: W. W. Norton and Company, 1963), pp. 263-68.

psychological needs in some way, at the risk of otherwise impairing human personal development.

It may be thought that the celibate can or does meet fully all these needs in a relationship to God. But although God may be a "significant other" in the celibate's life—in some ways more significant than in the life of other people—still the celibate must meet these psychological needs in relationships with other men and women in some measure. He or she needs to have companions, cultivate friends, care for others and be cared for, occasionally exchange confidences with someone, and contribute to the life and growth of the next generation and society. Jesus himself did not live entirely without these human helps and satisfactions. Monasticism, even in its more rigorous forms, provides for them in some way. The isolated hermitage is for the man or woman who first reaches spiritual maturity in the context of community. Moreover, Christian faith maintains that our relationship to God is expressed and lived out in our relationship to neighbors. And let us admit it, some "saints" are queer people because they neglected or condemned these psychological needs; or in some cases the populace has mistakenly regarded neurotics as saints.

The adventure in celibacy does not consist, as some suppose, in bearing unfulfilled needs, namely, want of a loving and understanding spouse to assist in life's trials; want of genital sexual pleasure; want of companionship, love, cherishing, intimacy, parenthood. The adventure consists in satisfying the human needs for all these things in virtuous ways other than through marriage. The celibate ventures into community living and friendship of varying degrees to fulfill the human need for companionship, loving and being loved, cherishing and being cherished, intimacy, and support in life's trials. The celibate embarks upon service to others in sublimation of the need for genital sexuality and in fulfillment of the need for generativity. The celibate strives for a deeper relationship with God, partially because he or she experiences a thrust toward that goal, but partially in order to fulfill at a deeper level or in a more comprehensive way those human needs which have been mentioned.

The struggles of celibacy's adventure, therefore, are not primarily to suppress desires and endure privations, any more than the struggles of the adventure of climbing Mt. Everest are primarily establishing a base camp at the foot of the mountain. The struggles of celibacy's adventure are to actualize potentialities, fulfill longings, move forward and upward toward a fully satisfying human life in the likeness of Christ's life.

Celibacy's building of human life in Christ, like any other attempt at making a worthwhile life, is not one momentary struggle, but a series of efforts with some failures and some successes. The successes bring one ever closer to the goal. The endeavor to build a friendship will have its progress and reversals. It may fail and another entirely new attempt must be made. A friendship established may flounder over misunderstandings and will have to be restored to balance. The endeavor to sublimate the drive for genital gratification is sometimes easy and successful, at other times difficult and perhaps unsuccessful; a new strategy must be developed to achieve the goal—perhaps a change in work, or a greater dedication to work, or a renovation of the spiritual life. To satisfy the need for generativity one's service to others may have to be altered from time to time, new forms of service undertaken, with all the uncertainty, fears, and efforts that accompany change in our lives. As adventure is made up of a series of successes and failures, so is celibate life.

The adventure of celibacy involves periodic taking stock of the situation, of obstacles and opportunities for human growth. Imagination and ingenuity are called for to discern ways of meeting some keenly felt needs for fulfillment. Courage must be mustered and an attempt made to meet the need. If the attempt fails, a new tactic must be devised to overcome the frustration and move toward the goal. Again courage must be exercised and an effort made. When success in meeting one challenge is had, another challenge appears and the process of stocktaking, discerning, planning, generating courage, and trying will have to be repeated.

This repeated process usually goes on more or less naturally. The needs, and the drives to fulfill them, are in us and function without our being reflectively conscious of them. We do not set out to be open to, or to build friendships after long deliberation and consultation; we more or less spontaneously make friends. We do not usually debate with ourselves how to sublimate the desire for genital sexuality but naturally move toward absorbing service of others. We run into snags often enough, however, so that we become conscious of what is going on within us, we become aware of our striving and our frustration. In such instances we are compelled to reflect on, and become sensitive to, what is happening; we must deliberately intervene in the process after thoughtful planning and consultation with others. It may even be said that the more aware we are of this unfolding of the process toward human fulfillment in Christ, the more human is our adventure of celibacy. Such self-awareness, however, is not what is popularly referred to as "self-consciousness"; we do not go through the process of growing humanly in some wooden, logical, artificial manner. It remains a natural process; but we are aware of it, in some measure master of it, and able to appreciate the suffering and the joy it entails.

The outcome of celibacy is uncertain, in keeping with its quality of adventure. Uncertain it is whether the celibate will succeed in sublimating his or her drive for genital sexual pleasure. This uncertainty, however, is not the most substantial. More significant is the possibility that the celibate, unable to cope with frustrations in achieving the purpose for which celibacy was chosen, may become a very disgruntled, cynical person. Uncertain also is whether the celibate can provide for himself or herself at various stages of life adequate satisfaction of the psychological needs for companionship, exchange with the opposite sex, loving and being loved, holding and being held special, intimacy, and generativity, so that his or her personality development is humanly wholesome. The final uncertainty is whether the celibate will so negotiate the challenges to human development inherent in celibacy that he or she in old age will look back over his or her life and say of it: "It is consummated. I accept it, its limitations and sufferings as well as its richness and joy. I would not have it be other than it is. It is I. I am fulfilled and ready to meet my God." Successful **celibate** human development is not the only basis for such affirmation, of course, nor even the most important basis. But celibacy is an adventure precisely because it involves a risk that this affirmation could not be made at life's termination even though other facets of life were successful.

Celibacy, then, like adventure, means taking risks. There are the risks involved in attempting to meet various challenges throughout the course of life—challenges which, if not conquered, mean periodic or perpetual suffering and unhappiness. Supreme is the risk that, on the last day, one may not be able to say of one's life: "I accept it. I would not have it otherwise." Celibacy is high adventure, for the stakes are high: human fulfillment and happiness of a Christlike quality.

To begin and continue the adventure of celibacy requires daring, or readiness to take risks for the sake of reaching a worthwhile goal. It calls for courage, or strength of spirit, amid an onslaught of fears which would incline one to give up a worthwhile project. Patience is demanded, for the suffering involved in any struggle along the way has to be endured for some time. Because some of the sufferings must be endured for a considerable length of time, or because achievement of the goal entails repeated struggles with their accompanying suffering, perseverance is a requisite. It must be remembered, however, that the risk-taking, the facing of grave fears, the enduring of suffering in snatches or for a long time or repeatedly are not the substance of celibate life. That core is a positive thrust toward God and concern for fellow human beings. This substance is a source of enthusiasm, satisfaction, peace. The tenseness of daring, the conflict of courage against fears, the resistance of patience to suffering, or the weary efforts of perseverance to endure may occasionally overshadow the more positive feelings issuing from celibacy's substance, but these latter dominate in the long run.

Mountain climbers can look back with a profound sense of achievement, first from the base camp to the plain below, then to the previous camp from each camp site laboriously established ever higher on the slope. So also along the course of life the celibate can look back at various points with a sense of accomplishment. Perhaps he or she realizes one day that over the years greater mastery has been gained over tantalizing urges for genital sex. The celibate may recognize that a friendship has been established which provides satisfaction of the need for intimacy. A ministry, for which celibacy has allowed absorbing dedication, may be appreciated as a substantial contribution to the welfare and happiness of many people in the present and for the future.

Even in the midst of struggles there is a sense of achievement. Satisfaction springs from activity: from using personal ingenuity, strength, and determination;

from successful employment of external resources. The mountaineer senses he is very much alive as he carefully negotiates his way around an outcropping of rock, as he strains muscles to pull himself upward, as he pushes on in spite of an aching body. The celibate knows that he or she is very much alive in struggles with longings for companionship, with sexual yearnings both physical and psychological, with distracting forces of love, with self-emptying requirements of friendship, with urges to immortalize self in another generation—struggles not to suppress or destroy but to fashion a fulfilling human life.

The final achievement in the adventurous journey of celibacy is, of course, a fulfilled human life in Christ. By **fulfilled human life** is meant a life of which it can be said, as was mentioned above: "I accept it." It is not a life which has been without suffering, pain, agony, but a life in which, through these experiences, practical wisdom and compassion have been gained. It is a life in which human potentials have been actualized, human needs satisfied in ways fostering human dignity, and human drives employed to produce one's own welfare and others'. A fulfilled human life includes friendship developed through grace with God the Father, in Jesus Christ his Son incarnate, through the power of their indwelling Spirit. This relationship of grace is not tacked on to the human but permeates every fiber of it and qualifies the whole of it. Because of this relationship, what may appear to unbelieving eyes a defective life is, as a matter of fact, a fulfilled human life.

If a celibate person can see his or her celibacy, not as a deprivation to be endured, or a burden to be borne, but as an adventure in living humanly, celibacy stimulates life. There are fresh decisions to be made and new projects to be undertaken, in order to meet ever newly discovered challenges to human fulfillment. The vow or promise of celibacy does not put an end to choices, but provides a new horizon for countless other exercises of freedom. Because the outcome of each decision and project is uncertain and the risks are high, celibate life is exciting. Very often it will appear troublesome, but if one has vision, it will appear to be, rather than troublesome, actually exciting. Thus religious celibacy gives zest to life. It does not make life dull. It yields a sense of satisfaction along the way and eventually Christian and human fulfillment.

Chapter 5

FRIENDSHIP WITH GOD AND PRAYER

Two fundamental challenges confront a person in the adventure of celibate life. One challenge is to grow in communion with God. The other is to develop good relationships with people.

The first challenge is basic because, if it is not met, a major purpose of celibacy is not achieved. A person's conscious choice of celibacy may have been explicitly motivated by some other purpose than growing union with God, for example, freedom for ministry to a wide range of people, or witness to new life in the Spirit, or fulfillment of the Church's discipline for ordained ministers. But if increasing intimacy with God is lacking, authentic realization of these other intentions will not occur. The celibate will have little or nothing religious to bring to those to whom he or she ministers; or testimony to new life in the Spirit will be hollow; or fulfillment of the Church's discipline will be merely external, never attaining its purpose and value.

The development of human relationships is fundamental because without them the celibate will experience human unhappiness. This unhappiness will inhibit his or her witness to the joy found in communion with God. It may even prevent that communion and its satisfaction. Without the development of human relationships, moreover, the celibate will not be an effective minister of God's message and love. Such failure will only intensify dissatisfaction, with further adverse effects on the celibate's witness and ministry.

Communion with God is based on faith and hope and realized in charity, or Christian love. The human reality which Thomas Aquinas employs as a model or analogue to gain some insight into the mystery of Christian love of God is friendship: charity is a kind of friendship with God. **(Summa theologiae,** II-II, q. 23, a. 1). Of course, friendship with God differs in many respects from friendship with men and women, but friendship provides a category for conceiving of our relationship to God in charity.

The relationships with people to which we referred above can be designated friendships. These relationships are of various kinds, and some kinds often go by other names than friendship. For the present, however, we can group under the name friendship all those interpersonal relationships which involve some continuing mutual sharing of lives at one or another level of depth. This definition is vague and we will have to clarify it later, but it is sufficient to make a point here.

The point is that the fundamental challenges in the adventure of celibacy can be conceived as the cultivation of friendships—friendship with God and friendships with men and women. The struggles in which celibates engage are principally those of establishing and maintaining friendships. Their joys are those of friendship. Once again we see the positive thrust of celibacy. It is not chiefly a matter of resisting urges for physical sexual pleasure or of enduring without that gratification. Nor is it mainly a matter of persevering through life without any human relationships or with only superficial ones. It is, rather, a matter of developing a variety of friendships, divine and human. Through these friendships personality unfolds and expands, talents come to light, unrecognized potentialities are actualized, human needs are provided for, responsibility is developed, freedom of choice is evoked, loyalty is tested, Christian virtues are nourished, a realistic self-image emerges, and self-confidence is generated. The remainder of this book will concern friendships in the life of celibates—first friendship with God and then human friendships.

The idea of friendship with God, however, presents theological difficulties. It is too audacious. Friendship, at least its noblest form, implies equality of the partners in the sense that each, having something to give to the other, gives it, and each receives from the other, so that each is richer than he or she would be alone. A shared good or value underlies friendship, for example, an interest in literature, a concern for the environment, or an agreement about how to live a worthwhile life. Because people share common interests, concerns, and viewpoints they are drawn to one another, exchange thoughts and feelings with another about their common values, and engage in activities together to obtain, preserve, and increase the goods which unite them. But what have we to give to God who, as Absolute Plenitude of Being, lacks nothing? What common good or value can we finite creatures share with the infinite God? It would seem that in relation to God we can claim no more than utilitarian friendship on our side, that is, loving him for what he can do for us. On God's side, can he ever be closer to us than a father to his children?

We can and must understand our relationship to God in many ways, as Scripture testifies. We are, for example, creatures of the Creator, subjects of the King of the universe, dependents on the Provider, adorers of the Holy One, sinners before the Judge, and children of the Father. But the Gospel of John has Jesus say: "I no longer speak of you as slaves. . . . Instead, I call you friends. . . ." (John 15:15). St. Paul wrote: "God . . . called you to fellowship with his Son, Jesus Christ our Lord" (I Cor. 1:9). When Thomas Aquinas takes a suggestion from these passages and interprets the key Christian virtue of charity in terms of a kind of friendship with God, he leads us to contemplate a truly awesome aspect of the Christian mystery.

By grace God the Father, through his Son incarnate, Jesus Christ, by the power of the Holy Spirit, makes us sons and daughters by adoption. We become heirs with Jesus of the glory bestowed on him in his resurrection. We too become "sharers of the divine nature" (II Pet. 1:4). The good which the Father, Son, and Holy Spirit share, which they know, love, and rejoice in, namely, Divinity itself, is given to us, so that we too might know, love, and rejoice in it with the Father, Son, and Holy Spirit. That this gift of sharing in the very life and blessedness of the Trinity is intended for us is manifested in Jesus raised from the dead and glorified, the first-born of many brothers and sisters (Rom. 8:29).

We have, then, by grace, a good shared in common with the three divine Persons—the Godhead in all its richness of being, truth, goodness, beauty, and power. As this Godhead is at the heart of the life of the Father, Son, and Holy Spirit, so it is at the heart of our graced lives. Our sharing through grace in this common good with the Trinity is one basis for designating our relationship to God as a kind of friendship.

Amazingly, we have something to give to the three divine Persons relative to the common good which is the basis of friendship with them. They will to share with creatures the Divine Being, Truth, Goodness, Love, Beauty, Power which they are. Creation results from this divine choice. The Father through the Eternal Word by the power of the Holy Spirit brings out of nothingness myriad creatures which reflect various aspects of Divine Reality. To creatures endowed with spirit, the Trinity offers, not merely a finite participation in Divine Being, but themselves—Father, Son, and Spirit in their Godhead—as the term of spiritual creatures' knowledge and love and the fulfillment of their creaturely desires.

We can hinder, though not prevent totally, the Trinity's sharing their Being. We can destroy, disfigure, and abuse creatures. We can refuse that faith, hope, and love by which the Father, Son, and Holy Spirit are received into our lives as the fulfillment of our knowing and loving. We can place obstacles in the way of other men's and women's faith, hope, and love. Thus we can impede in some measure the diffusion of Divine Being, Truth, Goodness, and Beauty throughout creation. We can block to some extent the three divine Persons from sharing with us and other men and women their life centered in their Godhead: we can hinder friendship between them and us.

Conversely, enabled by grace, we can promote the sharing of Divinity. We can care for God's creatures and use them for the purposes for which they were created. We can cooperate with the Creator by human artistry and craft, making new creatures, so to speak, out of the raw materials provided by creation. We can contribute to the establishment of God's reign in men and women by announcing the Good News to them, encouraging and supporting their faith, hope, and love, securing justice for them, tendering them corporal and spiritual works of mercy. Thus we have something to give to the Father, Son, and Holy Spirit. We do not give it absolutely on our own, but by their grace. Yet it is truly our gift, issuing from our free will moved by their grace. We give the Persons of the Trinity their external glory, their reign, by our graced yet freely-given consent to, and cooperation with, their activity.

By our acceptance of the Trinity as our personal fulfillment, we contribute to their dominion over our lives, their glory realized in us. In addition, we join them in their project of sharing their Divinity with all creation and all women and men. In doing this, we satisfy God's will as well as our own needs. Although we benefit, we are doing the Beloved's will and not simply our own. We have then the requisites for a kind of friendship with the Father, Son, and Holy Spirit: a shared good—namely, the Divine Being, Truth, Goodness, Beauty, Power—and mutual love in regard to that common good, they giving it to us for our happiness and we, cooperating with their giving, giving them its glorification by creatures. Thus a kind of friendship with God, with the Persons of the Trinity, is theologically possible and called for by Christian revelation.

Nevertheless, friendship with God presents a psychological difficulty. A correlation exists between our image and acceptance of self and our image and acceptance of God. Our self-image can prevent us from regarding men and women as our friends: we can see little or no worth or lovableness in ourselves and consequently believe no one else can. We cannot accept or love ourselves, so we cannot conceive of anyone else's accepting or loving us. If we think of ourselves as essentially bad, forever failing, good for nothing but sinning, we inevitably conceive of God as someone who can only be angry with us or who, if he graciously forgives us, can still only be infinitely distant from us in his holiness and perfection. If we conceive of ourselves as constantly having to prove our worth by thinking, saying, and doing the right things, we will correspondingly think of God as an ever alert judge ready to accuse and condemn us. We may be able to talk eloquently about God as Friend: we may be able to expound the theology sketched above. But unless we have an image and acceptance of ourselves as intrinsically good and of worth, both as creatures and as graced creatures, we will not be able to regard God as **our** Friend.

The only answer to this psychological difficulty is, of course, the development of a healthy self-image and of self-acceptance in the realms of both nature and grace. Words alone, explanations alone, cannot produce this development. It can occur only in living through a variety of human experiences which go well from the standpoint of the kind of self-image and self-acceptance they beget. Often these experiences—for example, interaction with parents in infancy and childhood, initial years in school, adolescence—generate a poor self-image and a low self-esteem. If the outcome of these experiences is faulty, personal effort with the help of others is necessary to correct the image and achieve acceptance of self.

This need for a good self-image and for self-acceptance in order to regard God as Friend suggests that we should consider human friendships in celibates' lives before friendship with God. Until our human relationships have built up our self-esteem, how can we regard God as our Friend? Indeed, until we have good experiences of human friendship and so know experientially what friendship entails, how can we enter into friendship with God?

In treating friendship with God at this point we are not saying that it must be chronologically first in celibates' lives. The suggestion is not being made that celibates should refrain from developing human friendships until they feel friendship with God has been established. There are at least two reasons for not making such proposals.

One reason is that friendship with God is a growing relationship throughout life. We may be able to point to a span of time in which we began to see and feel our relationship to God as friendship rather than only inferiority, subjection, condemnation, or childhood. But it is difficult to recognize a moment in which we can say that friendship with God is definitively established and we are now ready for human friendships.

Another reason for not saying that friendship with God must be temporally first is that growth in the relationship to God and development in relationships to men and women are correlative. In struggling with friendships at various levels with men and women, we learn much about how to love God and be loved by him. As we love another person through various disappointments in regard to our expectations of what we would gain from the friendship, we discern the selflessness which should characterize our love for God; and we appreciate the generosity of God's love for us who so often fall short of the discipleship to which he calls us in Christ. On the other hand, contemplating the revelation in Jesus Christ of God's love for us, and responding to his invitation to share his life, we discover much to help us in achieving genuine human friendships. Our trusting God, for example, even though we understand so little of his ways toward us, can teach us to trust our friends when their conduct toward us is incomprehensible. This trust in a time of crisis may be what is needed to preserve a threatened relationship.

Although friendship with God and friendships with women and men develop simultaneously and are mutually helpful, friendship with God has a primacy of presence, concern, and influence. God is always there to be the horizon of our lives, and our relationship to him is a continuing concern. People, on the other hand, pass in and out of our lives. Our relationships to most of them are of concern only for periods of time. As for those friends who remain in our lives, they too **can** pass on, even though neither we nor they wish or intend to part ways. Great as may be our concern for our relationships with these people, none of the relationships is our ultimate concern, as is our relationship to God. Striving above all else for deep friendship with God, moreover, strengthens celibates for intimate relationships with persons of either sex in ways consistent with celibacy. Friendship with God, therefore, makes possible a wide range of friendships for celibates. For these reasons, then, and not because friendship with God is necessarily prior in time to any human friendship, we treat first the relationship to God.

I would offer a hypothesis, however, namely, friendship with God will be temporally first in the lives of some people. Over the years of my ministry I have been impressed by the great number of people who cannot say "I'm O.K." and cannot, therefore, enter into human friendships. There do not appear to be enough vigorous, unselfish lovers in the world to beget self-accepting people in the first place and to heal all those who have grown up hating themselves.

God's intention revealed in Jesus Christ is to save us in the totality of our humanity from the evils which beset us. Among these evils must certainly be included that non-acceptance of self which causes so much misery in individuals and in interpersonal relationships. I suggest, therefore, that some people will achieve self-acceptance and hence the ability to enter into friendships with others only by first discovering that God accepts them, that therefore they are acceptable, and that God is their Friend. Their first or at least their most convincing experience of being accepted and hence of accepting themselves will come in the realization that God loves them infinitely, in spite of their shortcomings, even to his incarnate Son's dying to show that love. From this experience of God as Friend they will be able to form genuine human friendships.

One may insist that the first or most convincing experience of being accepted by God's love cannot occur except through the mediation of being accepted by human love. But this position, it seems to me, limits the power of God's grace of salvation in Jesus Christ. It means that if deeply rooted self-acceptance has been prevented by parents' failure to love in infancy and childhood, and if no healing human love has come forth thereafter, a person cannot be saved in this life from the evil of self-rejection; he or she is condemned to misery for the whole of his or her life.

I believe, on the contrary, that through the cultivation of the life of faith, especially prayer, some people can and will discover a loving God who accepts them—a discovery so profound that it will heal them of their self-rejection and enable them to establish friendships as they could not previously do. Such development, I grant, would normally depend upon their receiving kind, sympathetic, generous help from one or more persons. If this sort of help is what is meant by "human love mediating God's love," I am willing to grant the principle that God's love is normally mediated through human love. It seems more precise to me, however, to regard such help as something different than what we usually mean by human love, and to see it as disposing or opening a person for the discovery of God's love rather than mediating it in the strict sense.

I would add that such human help, however interpreted, would be normal, but not necessarily universal. If God's saving grace is truly all that it is said to be, the possibility must be left open for someone's coming to regard God as Friend prior to regarding any human being as friend. It may be in the agony of human rejection and isolation that one discovers God in the profoundest way and consequently discerns his or her own worth, so that he or she can go forth to be loved by others and to love them. Such an event may be rare, but it is not impossible.

Though we have justified friendship with God as a

theologically sound way of interpreting our relationship to God and have explained why we are considering that friendship before human friendship, we are still faced with a difficulty. God does not appear in our experience as do the persons with whom we establish friendships. He is not a visible, tangible reality like women and men. He does not engage in conversation with us. We never see, hear, or touch him. How can we experience friendship with the invisible, intangible, silent?

If the response to this difficulty is that we know God by faith in his revelation of himself, it must be admitted that the reality of God remains most obscure even to faith. God remains hidden behind the media—the personages, events, and words—by which he reveals himself. Our conceptualizations of God, based on his revelation, point to, but do not lay hold of, God; they do not deliver him over to us, so to speak, but direct us to him with more or less accuracy, and ultimately by saying more what he is not than what he is. How then can God be regarded as a friend like the human beings with whom we form friendships—very concrete realities who make an obvious impact on us? We are more inclined to think of, and relate to, God as some remote, hidden, vague, abstract ultimate power behind the universe of nature and grace rather than a vividly present personal being with whom we can live in friendship.

This difficulty does not preclude development of a sense of friendship with God; it merely offers a challenge. We can meet this challenge by practicing the prayer of presence which puts faith and love into action and yields a sense of God whereby we can relate to him as Friend. Let us unpack this last sentence.

We speak of "prayer of presence." That name I have chosen for the sort of prayer that will be described. In the literature of spirituality, other names have been given to this kind of prayer or, probably more accurately, its culmination: for example, active recollection, prayer of simplicity, simplified affective prayer, acquired contemplation. Whatever name is given to it, it approaches and becomes the final stage of prayer in which our effort is more obvious than the Holy Spirit's grace moving us to the prayer in which we are engaged. Beyond this sort of prayer, the Spirit's working is obviously dominant; we are "carried away" by the Spirit, experiencing what is called infused contemplation.

The different names for this kind of prayer or its culmination signify diverse aspects of it. "Prayer of simplicity," for example, indicates that it is not complex reasoning or a stream of words interior or exterior; "simplified affective prayer" points to the quality of this prayer on its emotional or volitional side. I have chosen "prayer of presence" to emphasize that this prayer is in the presence of God envisioned as Personal Being, as Friend. It is prayer seeking intensified awareness of God's presence and desiring union of mind and heart and being with him so present.

The prayer of presence begins with an act of the faith whereby we live our daily Christian lives. By this act of faith we place ourselves in the presence of God or, more precisely, in the presence of the three divine Persons: Father, Son, and Holy Spirit.

By faith we affirm belief that God is Personal Being, not merely an impersonal force or power or ground of being. We believe in response to the revelation witnessed in the Scriptures and Christian tradition that God knows, loves, and cares for his creatures and especially human beings as much as, indeed more than, any person in our experience knows, loves, and cares for what he or she begets or makes. We so believe even though we do not understand how God knows, loves, and cares in most cases: God's ways are not our ways.

Our faith in God's revelation in Jesus Christ especially convinces us that God is Personal Being. We have Jesus' teaching that God is his Father and ours, that the Father knows the secrets of our hearts, loves all men and women including those who do not obey him, and provides for our needs even as he does for the lilies of the field and the birds of the air. More significantly still, Jesus appears to us as a person such as we meet in our own experience, but Christian reflection on him has led to the realization that his personhood is ultimately divine. In Jesus, God is most certainly revealed as personal, that is, as possessing those characteristics required of a friend, though he possesses them in a manner infinitely superior to that of any human person and infinitely beyond our ability to know them, except through analogy or symbolism which accurately points to them.

Christian faith professes, moreover, an astounding richness to God's personal quality: God is three persons— Father, Son and Holy Spirit—in one divine nature. **Person** is generally understood today in a different sense than that intended in this formula as it was hammered out in the early history of Christian dogma. Then it had a metaphysical sense; now we give the word a psychological meaning. In its original sense the formula is intelligible, though it is difficult to understand and definitely impossible to imagine, or picture. The formula becomes even more challenging to intelligence when we attempt to account for it with the popular contemporary meaning of the word person. Theologians labor to interpret the formula in a way which respects its original meaning and at the same time makes sense today. The results of their efforts are difficult to follow but it is not necessary that we do so here. The point we wish to affirm now is simply that God is indeed a personal reality as much as, and more than, any of our friends. On this score at least, it is possible to relate to God in friendship.

Some theologians and Christian writers today speak

of God as Presence, the mysterious One we encounter beyond the surface realities of daily experience. They prefer to define God as Presence in order to suggest the personal quality of God. Because of this intent, the use of Presence as a name for God is welcome. I myself, however, find the word vague, unsubstantial, and, despite the intent of those who use it, impersonal. For me it is little better than naming God Force, or Power, or Ground of Being. I prefer to think of God as Personal Being. "Being" expresses God's realness, his substantiality, his independence, his plenitude of perfection; "Personal" indicates the fact that God as Plenitude of Being includes in a supereminent manner knowing, loving, caring, and receiving such as we require for friendship. I can relate to God as Personal Being in friendship.

At the beginning of the prayer of presence, then, we affirm belief in God as Personal Being, indeed triune Personal Being. But more activity of faith is required if this affirmation of belief is to enable us to regard God as Friend comparable to our human friends. By faith we have to think long and intensely of God as our Friend, so that this conception of God sinks into our minds, becomes our habitual vision of him, and constitutes the horizon on which we see all of life and make our choices. We have to move further into the prayer of presence.

This prayer now entails a firm but calm effort to be highly conscious, in faith, of God's reality, his intimate presence, his knowledge, love, and care for us, his eagerness to share his life with us and to receive our life from us. To stimulate and support our effort at intensified awareness of God we may use Scripture, the writings of saints or theologians, liturgical texts or rites, nature, or events in our own lives which speak of God as real, intimately present, knowing, loving, and so on. We may express, in thought and even words, praise and thanksgiving to God for his being all this, or we may petition him to continue being all this, or we may seek forgiveness for offenses against him.

Great care must be taken, however, not to let our thinking stop at the meaning of the Scriptures, the liturgy, and so forth. We must go beyond the meaning to the Meant, to God. If we become preoccupied with the meaning, we are studying Scripture, the liturgy, the writings of the saints, rather than using them as means or occasions for reaching spiritually for God himself. Similarly, if we terminate our thinking at words of praise, thanksgiving, petition, or contrition, we are composing sermons or prayers rather than seeking communion with God in prayer.

We can maintain the heightened orientation of our minds to God by constantly recalling ourselves from distraction to attend in the darkness of faith to the reality of the omnipresent, immanent, and transcendent God. This recalling to attention implies reminding ourselves that what we are seeking is not understanding of this passage of Scripture or this event of our lives but God to whom these things point; we are not seeking the most apt and exact expression of praise or petition but God to whom we are addressing our praise or petition.

Attending to God implies repeatedly reminding ourselves that he to whom we are striving to be united is beyond any words, images, ideas, thoughts, or feelings that we have. He whom we are seeking transcends any and every thing, even the loftiest idea or the most sublime feeling we may experience. He is also more immanent than our deepest feelings and our profoundest insights into world or self. None of these is God. For what we seek is the infinite God who is no-thing, but the Absolute Plenitude of Personal Being whom we can know in this life ultimately only by saying what he is

not, as Thomas Aquinas **(Summa theologiae, I**, q. 3, prologue) and John of the Cross **(Ascent of Mount Carmel,**
Bk. I, chap. 13) remind us.

Prayer of presence will tend, therefore, to rise beyond
consideration of Scripture, liturgy, devotional writings,
personal experience, nature, and beyond praise, thanksgiving, petition, in order to be aware of God in a "cloud
of unknowing." To be aware of God in this way is to be
spiritually reaching for him, that is, reaching for him by
interior acts of faith and love, while reminding ourselves that any image or thought or feeling of him which
we are having is not he.

We may, by the way, imagine that reaching as directed inward and downward to depths within us where
we enounter God in his immanence to us and the universe, or as directed outward, around, and upward where
God is found in his transcendence, or as directed in both
ways. How we imagine this reaching for God beyond
anything of which we are conscious is a matter of personal preference.

We should not be misled by the phrase "cloud of
unknowing" into thinking that this prayer consists in
some kind of trance, stupor, state of utter relaxation,
complete passivity, or suspended consciousness. Prayer
of presence does require slowing down our mental activities, going beneath or beyond or being detached from
irrelevant thoughts and images which pass through our
minds; it calls for pacifying our emotions and putting
our bodies in a place and position which facilitate spiritual tranquility. We do have to "pull ourselves together"
for this prayer. The religious traditions of both the West
and the East offer many methods for achieving such
peace and integrity. But all this negation of activity is
a condition for the prayer of presence, not its substance.
The latter is activity—spiritually reaching for God. Far
from being inertness, passivity, trance, suspended con-

sciousness, this prayer is heightened, intensified consciousness, but peaceful, not frenzied.

To know God in a cloud of unknowing, to be reaching for him beyond every idea and image, is not opposed to relating to him as Friend. God is beyond the idea of Friend, but the idea accurately points to what or who God is as he has revealed himself in Jesus Christ. Moreover, the idea enables us to relate ourselves to him as friends to Friend, although he is hidden in a cloud of unknowing. In other words, the idea of God as Friend is important both because it directs us to God in accord with his revelation and because it determines how we think and feel about ourselves in relation to him.

An essential ingredient of the activity involved in the prayer of presence is love for God in its aspect of desire to know him, to possess him and be possesed by him, to enjoy him and his presence. The desire imbedded in love for God is what moves faith to that long, intense thinking of God, that attending to God by incessantly reaching spiritually for him beyond any words, images, thoughts, or feelings. This desire is never satisfied. However lofty may be the prayer which is ultimately given to us as the fruit of our desire, God lies beyond that experience. Hence, the desire for him remains unfulfilled and continues to urge us on to seek him.

The desire we are speaking about here is one which we have to elicit under the influence of God's grace. In itself, it is not the kind of desire we feel but the kind we **will,** sometimes when our feelings are quite the contrary. God's grace, which enables us to will this desire, may also provide support for it in our feelings. But we do not sit around waiting for the desire for God to well up from within us without any effort on our part. Sometimes the Spirit of God will take the initiative obviously; we will experience ourselves drawn to prayer and even feeling inclined to it. But we cannot afford to wait for

these moments of obvious inspiration if our goal is to
relate to God in friendship. Presuming that God's grace
is at work in us and relying upon it, we proceed humanly, using our intelligence and will, in the hope that the
action of the Spirit latent in us will become manifest.

To proceed humanly means, concretely, that we set
time aside frequently and with regularity to engage in
this prayer of presence, to attend long and intensely to
God as we consciously desire him in love beyond any
thoughts or images of him. It also means that we seize
opportunities to attend to him for brief intense moments
in the course of a day's activities.

Often prayer of presence will appear to be utter failure. Practical concerns and worries will distract our
minds from reaching for God, and even from attention
to the Scriptures or prayers we employ to aid us. Or we
will become more fascinated by the Scriptures than by
the God of whom they speak, or more interested in the
prayers we say than in the God to whom they are addressed. From awareness of God prompted by events in
our own lives we will drift into reveries. Often we will
be unable to generate any sensible feeling for prayer;
we will even appear to lack the will to seek God. As a
result of these interferences and failures, we will be
tempted to write off as wasted the time spent in the practice of this kind of prayer.

But apparently futile prayer of presence must be distinguished from that which is really such. The latter is
willful indulgence in thinking about the events of the
day, planning for tomorrow, working out theological
answers to questions, composing well-worded prayers,
daydreaming, or dozing. The prayer of presence involves
renewed efforts to be consciously desirous of God, to
reach spiritually for him beyond words, images, and
ideas, whenever awareness dawns that attention has
drifted away from God to creatures. If the thoughts

which have arisen are truly important and worth having, efforts are made to relate them to God—not the idea of God but God himself—at least by pondering them with willed effort at simultaneous consciousness of God's personal presence. Most often prayer of presence will repeatedly slip into distraction and have to be renewed again and again. Patience and perseverance are necessary to continue the process for an allotted time.

The temptation to be discouraged by this sort of experience is very great. We think nothing is being accomplished because we do not manage to reach a level of sustained attention to God undisturbed by any extraneous thoughts and oblivious to the world around us. Such prayer is a goal, but we must recognize humbly that it is a lofty one, attained only with time and self-discipline nourished by grace, and even then our role is not to achieve it but to dispose ourselves for God's gift of it.

Because our role in grace is a dispositive rather than an accomplishing one, however, prayer of presence is very effective even when it is a repeated recalling from distraction to attention to God and desire for him. It is doing, with grace, what we can do to attain communion with God, namely, opening ourselves to what God wishes to accomplish finally in us. If we do not engage in this sometimes laborious, often apparently futile prayer of presence, we cannot expect to experience the ideal prayer which God inspires only in a prepared spirit.

Prayer of presence perseveringly engaged in complements faith whereby we affirm that God is Personal Being. It complements faith in the sense of putting faith into action. Instead of simply affirming that God is Personal Being, we act toward him as such in the prayer of presence. We attend to and desire him as Personal Being in a manner analogous to the way we attend to and desire people as personal beings. As a result, the affir-

mation of faith becomes less abstract, less a proposition
in our mind about God, and represents what God really
is for us—Personal Being. That is how we treat him, so
that is how we come to regard him. Regarding him as
such, we more readily treat him as such. Although God
does not appear in our experience with the concreteness
of human persons, thanks to the prayer of presence he
is not only an idea, an abstraction, or a remote impersonal
force or ground. Through such prayer God becomes
impressively present to us as Personal Being to whom
we can relate in friendship.

Frequent prayer of presence not only makes God a
more vivid reality to us at certain times, but conditions
our minds and hearts so that God becomes the habitual,
at least implicit horizon of all our thoughts, desires, and
actions throughout our days. Or to use another figure of
speech, God is always "in back of our minds" as we go
about our daily affairs. Sometimes this habitual awareness of God becomes quite explicit even though we are
occupied with thoughts, desires, and actions centered
upon creatures. This presence of God through at least
implicit habitual awareness of him influences our decisions and conduct. Prayer of presence thus leads to living
continuously in consciousness of the presence of God,
our Friend.

The prayer of presence is the deep core of all the
forms of prayer which we initiate with the help of God's
grace. It is the goal toward which we aim when we take
up those forms of prayer. Meditation in the strict sense
is thinking about some element or aspect of the Christian
mystery in an orderly way leading to some practical
conclusion for one's life. But the practice of meditation
is meant to lead the spirit eventually to a quiet attending
to God with desire for him beyond all thoughts, images,
affections, and resolutions. If one is moved in the course
of meditation to pause and dwell upon God personally

present, one should not attempt to continue the thinking process in order to complete further steps of the meditation.

Mental prayer is any form of prayer which is carried on interiorly rather than expressed. It differs from meditation in the strict sense because it does not observe a method; it does not follow an orderly procedure of acts of imagination, faith, affection, application to one's life. It is spontaneously now adoring God, now praising him, now petitioning him, now expressing trust in him, now thanking him as one is inclined. But at the depths of this prayer, too, there is meant to be simple attending to God and desiring him in the darkness of faith beyond all the interior thoughts, images, feelings. The interior stream of words and affections should be set aside or ignored if one feels moved to rest in simple communion with God beyond all that "babble."

The core of vocal and liturgical prayer is likewise prayer of presence. The words, actions, and symbols of vocal and liturgical prayer are meant to focus our minds and hearts on God but in order to commune with him as he is beyond words, images, and ideas. Such communion with God, when it occurs, makes vocal and liturgical prayer profound spiritual experiences. The same must be said for spiritual reading or **lectio divina,** for informal group prayer and charismatic prayer, and for prayer through writing out one's reflections.

There is, then, a continuity between all the various forms of prayer we engage in. They all aim at what we have called the prayer of presence. They reinforce one another in our effort to pray simply in the presence of God vividly experienced, though experienced as beyond what we are conscious of. Vocal, liturgical, informal, communal, and charismatic prayer, spiritual reading, and prayer through writing aid us in putting our minds and hearts on God. They feed us with appropriate words, images, ideas which can be jumping off points for reaching spiritually for God in a cloud of unknowing. Meditation and mental prayer offer more freedom to reach spiritually for God because they are not linked to a train of words, actions, images, and feelings externally imposed by the liturgy, other people's vocal prayers, or some other source. We are more likely to arrive at sustained prayer of presence in meditation, and especially in mental prayer, than in externally expressed forms of prayer. These latter are necessary, however, to build up a world of faith which can be the milieu and the basis for reaching spiritually for God in the prayer of presence. In these external forms of prayer we are more likely to experience moments of the prayer of presence if we have practiced such prayer frequently, regularly, and faithfully.

So far we have seen that we can have friendship with God. Such a relationship is theologically possible and indeed called for by God's revelation in Jesus Christ. The psychological obstacles to regarding God as Friend can be overcome through life's experiences (perhaps corrected with the help of friends or professional counselors) and through the practice of the prayer of presence. But as Christians our friendship is not simply with God but with the Father, Son, and Holy Spirit. Our prayer, too, seeks communion with the three divine Persons. So we need to look into our relationship to the Trinity in friendship and prayer. We also need to consider further the content which our prayer may sometimes have. These matters are topics for the next chapter.

Chapter 6

THE TRINITY AND PRAYER

Several years ago I became aware of a great gap between my spiritual world of prayer and my Christian profession of faith. According to the latter, the God I proclaimed to believe in as Eternal Reality, Creator of everything that exists, and my personal ultimate goal and happiness, is Father, Son, and Holy Spirit. The Nicene Creed, which I recited most Sundays of the year, professes belief in Father, Son, and Holy Spirit who are somehow really distinct from one another, though only one God. The catechisms, religion books, and theological treatises in which I had been schooled presented the doctrine of the Trinity as the Christian conception of God. Even newer approaches to the exposition of Christian doctrine beginning with reflection upon Jesus Christ lead to the Trinity as the Christian understanding of God. The history of Christian doctrine, especially in the third and fourth centuries, testifies that Christian faith does not merely understand God to be three divine Persons in the sense that we look upon God in three different ways, but that this understanding reflects what or who God is. Though the word **person** in these early doctrinal developments and in later theological usage carried different overtones of meaning than we give to the word nowadays, the doctrine of three Persons in one God is a

basis for thinking of God as Them and not merely Him
or Her.

In my spiritual world, on the other hand, the Father,
Son, and Holy Spirit were not very distinct. Jesus, the
Son of God incarnate, was quite distinct because his
humanity makes him so obviously different from the
Father and the Holy Spirit. But when I thought of his
divinity, he became somewhat lost in the Godhead to
whom I related as the Ultimate Reality in whom my
happiness and the world's fulfillment is to be found. I
knew theoretically that this God is three divine Persons,
but practically I related to a Him rather than a Them.
The theological definition of the divine Persons as sub-
sisting relations did not, of course, provide much of substance to enable me to relate to a Them. Father, Son, and
Holy Spirit were three names which did not mean very
much to me in my everyday spiritual life, even though
I prayed many times every day: "Glory to the Father,
and to the Son, and to the Holy Spirit."

I began to be concerned that my world of prayer provided little place for a doctrine which had once been the
Church's major concern leading to ecumenical councils,
which men and women had fought and suffered over,
which had been expounded at great length in theology,
which constitutes distinctively Christian dogma about
God, and which repeatedly occurs in the liturgy. If I
was building my relationship to God on an interpersonal
model of friendship, then it was important to make the
Father, Son, and Holy Spirit vivid persons in my life.
I should think of God not as my Friend but as my Friends.

How can we make the Father, Son, and Holy Spirit
more vivid persons in our lives? A first step, I found, is
to begin to pray with a consciousness of their reality.
We may not understand how God is three divine Persons
and still only one God, but our faith affirms the real
distinctness of the Father, Son, and Holy Spirit who are

nevertheless one God. We can put faith into action by consciously reaching spiritually in the prayer of presence for God precisely as Father, Son, and Holy Spirit. When we think of friendship with God, we think of our friendship extending to three divine Friends who share the one Godhead. The one love, mercy, forgiveness, inspiration, and help which we contemplate and feel, we attend to as coming from three Persons, not just one Person.

We can take as a rough model the love and care which a family might give us. Though the family consists of many members, we may experience one love extended to us. We do not think of an invitation to dinner as coming only from the husband or only from the wife, or as two invitations, but one invitation from both. Their greeting at the door we accept as one welcome, even though it comes from two persons. The Trinity and its actions are very different from a family and its activities. Still, our experience with the latter can help us to think of ourselves as relating in prayer and in life to the Father, Son, and Holy Spirit as three distinct Persons, even though the love they give us and the source of that love are shared by them in common.

A second step to make the three divine Persons more vivid is to reflect on what Scripture, the liturgy, and theology attribute to each of them. A classical theological axiom states that any divine activities or their effects outside the Trinity involve all three Persons. The divine Persons are distinct only in their interrelationships. They are not distinct from the divine nature itself, which is one. It is necessary to maintain this axiom lest we fall into tritheism—three Gods rather than one God. Any divine activity of a divine Person outside Trinitarian relationships proceeds from the one divine nature with which all three Persons are identified. Thus, in the final analysis, the Trinity creates, redeems, and sanctifies.

Nevertheless, the New Testament as well as the litur-

gy and theology attribute, or appropriate, certain divine
actions and effects to the Father, others to the Son, and
still others to the Holy Spirit. For example, since the
Father is the Origin without origin in the Trinity—
source of the Son as well as, with the Son, of the Spirit—
the act of creation calling beings out of nothingness is
appropriated to the Father rather than to the Son or the
Spirit. Redemption is attributed to the Son, since the
Trinity's plan and performance of redemption was carried out in the human nature which he alone assumed
into the unity of his person. Sanctification is attributed
to the Holy Spirit, for sanctity consists essentially in love,
and the Holy Spirit is the personified love of the Father
and the Son. More specific activities and effects can, of
course, be appropriated to the various Persons of the
Trinity.

Such appropriation of divine activities and effects is,
in some measure, a manner of speaking, in accord with
the theological axiom noted above. It is a manner of
speaking, however, based on some kinship between the
unique character of the divine Person spoken of and a
particular activity or effect, as the examples above illus-
trate. This appropriation is, therefore, certainly more
than arbitrary. It is valuable practically for our spiritual
lives because it enables us to form a distinct idea for
each of the divine Persons, so that we can relate ourselves
to each of them.

Contemporary theologians tend to say that we have
some objectively distinct relationships to the different
Persons of the Trinity which are more than appropria-
tions, more than manners of speaking, even with some
foundation in reality. All divine activities and effects
come from all three divine Persons because of their identity in one divine nature. But the results of the divine
activity and aspects of these results are grounds for distinct real relationships to different Persons. For example,

all three divine Persons sanctify us through the one divine nature and activity, so that we are really related in dependence on all three Persons—Father, Son and Holy Spirit—as the effective source of our sanctification. But the model of our sanctification is the Son, for our sanctification occurs in human existence and only the Son among the three divine Persons was and is incarnate; only the Son is the exemplar for our holiness, not the Father nor the Holy Spirit. We are, therefore, objectively really related to the Son in a way we are not related to the Father or to the Holy Spirit.

This sort of thinking is indeed abstruse and we do not intend to pursue it. We have taken note of it to indicate that we are not indulging in fancy when we seek to make the three divine Persons more vivid as distinct from each other, so that we can relate to each of them as Friend. Though they are one God, the Father, Son, and Holy Spirit are not to be confused with one another; and we can learn to appreciate them and relate to them as such by attention to Scripture and liturgy, and by the prayer of presence guided by these sources.

In regard to Scripture, Karl Rahner has an essay entitled "**Theos** in the New Testament."[1] Rahner's thesis is that the word **God** in the New Testament usually signifies the Father and not simply the one Godhead common to all three Persons of the Trinity. The chief exception is instances when Christ is asserted to be God. With this thesis in the background, we can build up an idea of the Father by noting carefully, as we read Scripture, what activities and effects the New Testament attributes to the Father and also to God. We can also examine the New Testament for the activities and effects which are ascribed to the Son, the Word. Jesus Christ, and the

---

1—*Theological Investigations*, I (Baltimore: Helicon. 1961).

Spirit, or Advocate. Seeing these relationships between certain activities and effects on the one hand and, on the other, the different Persons of the Trinity is especially helpful in passages where two or three of the divine Persons are mentioned. Some such passages would be the prologue to the Gospel according to John (11-18); Christ's last discourse in the same Gospel (chaps. 14-17); Paul's reflections on Christian life (Rom. 8), revelation (I Cor. 1:6-16), Christ as the first fruits of salvation (I Cor. 15:2-28), sonship in God (Gal. 4:1-7), and the divine plan of salvation (Eph. 1-3).

Though nothing can substitute for personal study of such passages of the New Testament and prayer of presence arising from them, help can be gained from entries under "God," "Father," "Son," "Jesus Christ," "Holy Spirit," and the like in dictionaries of the Bible. We need not be scrupulous about theological precision in the connections we make, nor overly concerned about distinctions between Christ's divine, human, and theandric actions. Important, rather, is acquiring some distinctive notions of the Father, Son, and Holy Spirit which enable us to sense ourselves relating to each of them rather than to some blurred divinity.

The liturgy of the Roman rite is a veritable school of Trinitarian thinking. As Cyprian Vagaggini clearly and forcefully demonstrates in chapter seven of his **Theological Dimensions of the Liturgy,**[2] everything is envisioned in the prayers of the Roman rite as proceeding from the Father and to him, through the Son, in the Holy Spirit. The prayers of the Roman rite are normally addressed to the Father through the Son in the Holy Spirit. As Vagaggini shows, this vision of reality and this pattern of prayer are Scriptural. We can grow quickly in

---

2—(Collegeville: Liturgical Press, 1977).

appreciation of the three divine Persons as distinct Friends in our lives by sensitivity to the liturgy's manner of prayer and by assimilating its vision and pattern into our own prayer.

The question sometimes arises about what one is supposed to do in prayer. One activity appropriate to prayer is the effort to be conscious of the Father, or the Son, or the Holy Spirit as a distinct divine Person, to reach spiritually for one or the other, on the basis of our state of soul at the time and some divine activity or effect familiar to us and attributed by Scripture and the liturgy to that particular person. For example, when we are very conscious of the fragility of our existence, aware that we could cease to be, we can reach spiritually for the Father, the Source, the Origin, of our lives and of all creation, the Origin even of the Son and Holy Spirit within the Godhead. Feeling anxiety, guilt, shame, alienation, we can attend to the Son who has accomplished in his human life and death our ultimate salvation from threatening evils of every kind. If we feel distant from God and arid in prayer, we can reach in faith and desire for the Holy Spirit, whom the Father and Son send into our hearts and who prays within us (cf. Rom. 8:26).

Such prayer is like taking time out to appreciate one of our friends, that is, to note his or her particular qualities and traits which attract us and enrich us. We could probably afford to do this sort of thing more often in regard to each of our human friends. It would surely increase the joy we have in them by making us more conscious of the good in them. So prayer attending to each of the divine Persons helps us to form a distinct notion of each, increase our appreciation of each, relate ourselves to each, and enjoy more our friendship with each. As each of the divine Persons becomes more vivid to us in his distinctiveness, we find ourselves more often spontaneously praying to the Father, Son, and Holy

Spirit, rather than simply to God, and we think of ourselves as relating in friendship to three divine Friends.

In this reaching for the Father, the Son, and the
Holy Spirit in their distinctiveness we still must bear in
mind that their divine reality is beyond any images,
conceptions, or notions we have of them. This fact may
seem to cancel our attempts to relate to each of them
distinctly. If they, like the Godhead with which they are
identified, are known only in a cloud of unknowing, how
can we approach them in their positive distinctness?

The answer to this dilemma is that the distinct realities of the Father, Son, and Holy Spirit are indeed beyond the words, images, and notions we have. But the
distinct ideas we have provide us with a starting point
and orientation for our prayer and our relating to God—
a starting point and orientation in accord with the divine
revelation professed in Christian faith. Our distinct notions of the Persons of the Trinity do not do something
to the Father, Son, and Holy Spirit, namely, put them
in our mental grasp; rather, they do something to us,
namely, direct our prayer and our attitude of friendship
to them as distinct from each other. The experience into
which we will eventually be borne lies beyond the words,
images, and ideas with which we begin. Our role is, as
we have noted before, to dispose ourselves for the Divine
to invade our lives in a manifest way. Since the Divine
is revealed in Jesus Christ as Father, Son, and Holy
Spirit, it behooves us to open ourselves to it as such.
Our inadequate but accurate notions based on revelation
enable us to be open in this way.

Jesus Christ is indispensable in relating to the Father,
Son, and Holy Spirit in friendship and prayer. Jesus is,
of course, the Son incarnate, not simply God but God-
man, whose humanity is like ours in all things but sin and
is not to be confused with his divinity, however intimately related it is. Jesus as Son incarnate reveals in a pre-

eminent way the qualities of the Godhead of the three divine Persons with whom we are friends and for whom we reach spiritually in prayer—qualities of loving kindness, fidelity, compassion, care, forgiveness, justice. Prayerful reflection on Jesus is like spending time with our friends in order to know them better, discover their lovableness, and so love them more intensely.

Jesus reveals not only the Godhead but also the divine Son in his uniqueness, for he is the divine Son. In revealing the divine Son, Jesus also reveals in their uniqueness the Father who begets him as Son and the Holy Spirit who proceeds from him and the Father in their mutual love. In his humanity Jesus reflects the characteristics of the Son vis-à-vis the Father in the one Godhead: everything he has is from the Father and he returns everything to the Father. As he is in his humanity, so he is in a still more eminent way in his divinity: wholly from the Father, belonging totally to the Father, perfectly reflecting the Father, so much so that he is identical with the Father except for being from the Father, and the Father is identical with him except for being his origin.

In his glorified humanity, moreover, Jesus sends the Holy Spirit into the hearts of men and women. In sending the Spirit he again reveals his role as Son in the Godhead: with the Father, the Son breathes forth the Holy Spirit of the Father's and Son's mutual love. The Spirit is thus not the Father, nor the Son, for the Spirit is from them, while they are not from him. Yet what the Spirit brings to men and women is simply what he has from the Son, who has what he has from the Father. Correspondingly on the divine plane, the Holy Spirit has the same Godhead which the Father and the Son share; he is equally God with the Father and the Son, differing from them only in proceeding from them.

Prayerful reflection on Jesus, his life, death, resurrec-

tion, glorification, and sending of the Spirit leads, therefore, beyond his humanity, not simply to God, but to the
ineffable life of the Father, Son, and Holy Spirit, distinct
persons in the one God, as Edward Schillebeeckx strikingly shows in his book **Christ the Sacrament of the
Encounter with God.**[3] Jesus is the avenue to the Trinity
and thus to friendship with the Father, Son, and Holy
Spirit and to the prayer of presence reaching for them
by faith and desire in a cloud of unknowing.

When we reach for the Father, Son, and Holy Spirit
in a cloud of unknowing in the prayer of presence, we
reach beyond words, images, and ideas, as we have said
many times. We also reach beyond the humanity of
Jesus, which, like words, images, ideas, is finite, creaturely, indescribably different and distinct from the Godhead. But if we pass beyond the humanity of Jesus, we
do not pass beyond his person. On the contrary, we reach
for Jesus precisely as the Son of God, eternally begotten
by the Father and with the Father breathing forth the
Holy Spirit. Hence our prayer rises from and through
awareness of Jesus in his humanity to reach spiritually
for him as divine Son with the Father and the Holy Spirit. Christian mysticism, therefore, does not by-pass Jesus
Christ but reaches into the depths of his being to attain
him as the only begotten Son of the Father in the unity
of the Holy Spirit.

The three Persons as one God are the Subsistent Fullness of Being by and in whom everything lives, moves,
and has its being. If on occasion we are moved to prayer
of presence by the wonders of nature, the beauty of persons, the events of history, or the experiences of life, the
God we are inspired to reach for in faith and desire is
the God whom we know as Father, Son, and Holy Spirit

3—(New York: Sheed and Ward, 1963), pp. 25-39.

through revelation in Jesus Christ. Christian mysticism's roots, from which it incessantly draws life, are faith in Jesus Christ.

Jesus is crucial for Christian prayer and mysticism not only because he is the avenue to the depths of life in the triune God but also because he is the answer to prayer. He is the Word who is uttered in our minds by the Father for our understanding and wisdom. He is the Word to whom the Spirit bears testimony in our hearts and whose teaching the Spirit clarifies for us. We are transformed by prayer, even and especially by that prayer in which we go beyond words, images, thoughts, and desires and are met by God in what is a cloud of unknowing. We are tempted to think of such prayer as formless, void, empty, incapable of yielding any answers to us, any guidance for us, in the particularities of human existence. But not so, for in such prayer the Father speaks to us his Word, Jesus, and the Spirit testifies to him as our Savior. Eventually prayer yields the answer to all our needs—Jesus illuminated by the testimony of the Holy Spirit within us.

That last sentence may sound merely pious, and perhaps it is to many. But rather than pious, it is profound. It reaches into the depths of who Jesus is and what we derive from our prayer. We do indeed have to supply for our own needs the best we can, not looking for miracles from God. But the model for our endeavor and the end we hope to achieve by it is Jesus Christ. He is also the power behind our effort and its achievement. He is their goal. Even our attempt to establish a society of peace and justice begins and ends with him, the head of all humanity. Through Jesus we encounter the Father and through Jesus the Father speaks to us in our every need. For the person of prayer such affirmation is not pious talk or expected theological jargon but an expression of experience.

When the Father, Son, and Holy Spirit become vivid Persons to us and we relate to them as real Friends in our lives, we readily spend time and converse with them, as we do with human friends. This spending time and conversing with our divine Friends is prayer in its various forms. We can learn what its content may sometimes be by comparing it with the conversation we have with human friends in the time we spend with them.

A frequent tendency is to think of prayer as saying **nice** things to God or thinking edifying thoughts in the divine presence. To pray is to recall the Trinity's wonderful works for humanity in the history of salvation. It is to praise the Father for his power, wisdom, and providence and to thank him for sending his only begotten Son, Jesus Christ, for our redemption and his Holy Spirit for our sanctification. Prayer is the expression of faith, hope, and love. It is beautiful thoughts inspired by passages in Scripture or spiritual books. To pray is to petition the Father, Son, and Holy Spirit for the salvation of men and women, for the vitality of the Church, for the health and holiness of loved ones. Prayer is the experience of awe, reverence, admiration, humility, filial obedience, noble desires, peace.

As content for prayer all this is excellent. But if this is all that we judge appropriate content for prayer, it may be doubted that we often pray with the deep conviction and feeling with which the Psalmist or Jeremiah or Jesus prayed. Real prayer is not always pretty; it can be a cry to God in anguish or in anger. Real prayer is not dispassionate; it can be a song of joy and triumph.

In a good marriage, a husband can be himself with his wife with minimal fear of being rejected or deemed silly. He does not talk to his wife only about beautiful and inspiring topics. He does not always praise and thank her. The concerns which he discloses to her are not limited to the general needs of humanity or society. He speaks to her about his doubts, anxieties, anger, misery. Sometimes he complains about the way she acts. He expresses his concerns about affairs where he works, the condition of the house, the development of their children. He manifests to her his feelings of tenderness and his carnal desire. Similarly a wife in a good marriage can be herself with her husband; she does not need to play a role in his presence.

To be ourselves in the security of known and felt acceptance and love is an important, perhaps even necessary, means to the preservation of mental health and to growth in personal maturity. Potentially destructive feelings are not suppressed or repressed but expressed. The expression is preferably in a civil manner, but the glory of a good marriage or friendship is that even irrational expression can be absorbed by spouse or friend in love and forgiveness. Through self-revelation and the dialogue which it begets with spouse or friend, we discover what is in us, who we really are. This discovery, or clarified apprehension, of deeper levels of self makes it possible to counteract weaknesses, draw on strengths, achieve a realistic self-image with appropriate self-esteem and self-confidence, and thus be able to love others generously.

As a husband discloses himself to his wife, so we can express ourselves to the Father, Son, and Holy Spirit in prayer. We can speak to them about our doubts and convictions, our misery and our happiness. To them we can mention our dislikes and hostile feelings, knowing that they will not condemn us and we can ask for the healing of these attitudes, or at least the ability to live with them in ways which will not harm God's reign in us or in others. In prayer we can vent our disappointments and hurts, or savor our hopes and triumphs, without feeling that we will be judged damnable or vain. We can tell the Father, Son, and Holy Spirit how annoyed we are by someone, or how vexed we are that plans for the future have been thwarted. In the presence of the three divine Persons we can rehearse a joyful visit we had with a friend or review the remarkable success of a project we had undertaken. We can thank the Trinity for their many blessings but we can also complain to them about our sufferings.

Thus the stuff of prayer is not only the sacred, lofty, beautiful, and inspiring but also the mundane, prosaic, sometimes ugly, messy, and painful. If there is any doubt about the suitability of all this content for prayer, a reading of the psalms will quickly dispel the doubt. The psalms not only praise God for his wonderful works of creation and his care for his people. They also thank him for temporal survival and for family; and they lament at length over personal or collective misery, though in hope and confidence that he will rescue those who revere him. Jesus' prayer in the garden of Gethsemani also teaches us that the content of prayer is sometimes anguish over the evil which threatens or befalls human existence.

The ordinary affairs and anguishing trials of our lives are not the noblest content of prayer. Simple loving awareness of, and desire for, the Father, Son, and Holy Spirit in faith, hope, and charity remain the goal of the prayer we undertake with the help of grace. But sometimes we can pray at all only by assuming daily events and struggles into our prayer. We are so preoccupied with a task we have to perform, a hurt we have received, a concern about a friend, anger at some provocation, or joy over some success, that we find it impossible to praise and thank God for his more general gifts or to sympathize with the needs of others and intercede for them. We find it impossible to engage in the prayer of presence —to pass beyond words, images, thoughts, and feelings to reach in faith and love's desire for the Father, Son, and Holy Spirit in a cloud of unknowing. On the contrary, our minds are filled with words, images, thoughts, and feelings from which we cannot extricate ourselves.

But we can come before the Father, Son, and Holy Spirit with all our concern and let it play itself out in their presence. We can talk to them about it, as a husband would talk to his wife, or vice versa. Periodically in this sort of prayer we have to remind ourselves that we are in the Trinity's presence and offer our preoccupation to them; we need to ask them for their help to appreciate our concern if it is beautiful and joyful, or to bear it if it is ugly and painful. Sometimes in the course of such prayer we eventually see in perspective what we are praying about, reach beyond it to the Father, Son, and Holy Spirit, and experience the transcendent peace of the prayer of presence.

As full and honest self-revelation to his wife helps a husband to maintain mental health and grow in maturity, so prayer to the Trinity about everything in our lives aids our mental health and maturation. Instead of suppressing thoughts and feelings we express them to the Father, Son, and Holy Spirit. If we have a vivid sense of the three divine Persons as real Friends, and if periodically we consciously offer our thoughts and feelings to them for blessing or healing, this sort of prayer is truly expression of these thoughts and feelings, even though not to another human person. Through this kind of prayer we come to know better our aspirations and our fears, our strengths and weaknesses, our true worth, and especially the abiding, forgiving love which the Father, Son, and Holy Spirit have for us as we actually are, with our virtues and vices. This sort of prayer, therefore, can generate healthy self-esteem and self-confidence, so that we can love others more unselfishly.

Prayer of this kind I deem to have been especially important for my personal growth in the course of my

celibate life. I have not had at my side a marriage partner to whom many thoughts and feelings would have
been expressed. I have been separated from intimate
friends to whom I would have manifested them. I would
even propose the thesis that a way in which celibacy
fosters prayer is by putting a person in a situation in
which, if he or she is to express many thoughts and feelings, he or she is almost compelled to express them to the
Father, Son and Holy Spirit for lack of a human intimate
at hand. This thesis does not mean that celibates should
not have intimate friends to whom they can express
deeply personal thoughts and feelings; it means that very
often, if not usually, such friends are not as available for
talking as would be a spouse. Nor does the thesis mean
that celibates should attempt to solve through prayer all
the problems they experience. Prayer of the kind we have
been speaking about can be a subtle mode of suppression
or obsession and make problems worse rather than better.
But for celibates with balanced personalities, this sort of
prayer can be both significant prayer and a means of
growth in maturity.

Mere self-expression, of course, does not lead to maturity, but self-expression to which there is a response
from another self. A wife's expression of herself, for
example, evokes a response from her husband. He responds in silence or in words, favorably or unfavorably,
admitting and accepting, or challenging and refusing.
A wife's husband "talks back" in various ways. Dialogue
between two persons arises. As a result of the exchange,
the truth emerges into the light: what sort of person each
is, what motivates each, strong and weak points of character. The truth about herself the wife may not recognize in the course of the exchange but only afterwards
in reflection on what happened in it. Nor does the whole
truth emerge from one dialogue. It is only through repeated dialogue over the course of time that a wife has

the opportunity to understand herself better and to mature.

The analogous relation between wife and husband on the one hand and, on the other, the celibate and the Father, Son, and Holy Spirit appears to break down at this point: the Persons of the Trinity do not talk back. But they do! The three divine Persons talk back in revelation, in the external circumstances of life, and in our interior dispositions.

In revelation, the Father, Son, and Holy Spirit express the sort of persons they are, their motives, their designs. Important for the celibate, then, is continual searching in revelation, especially as found in Scripture, for the Trinity's response to what is in his or her mind and heart. In the external circumstances of life (living situation, duties, the claims made by others) and interior dispositions (strengths and weaknesses of character, interests and talents, fears and hopes), the Father, Son, and Holy Spirit also talk back to the celibate. Our adjustment to these circumstances and dispositions is our response to what divine Providence wills positively or permissively. By examining in prayer to the Trinity our current thoughts, feelings, desires, fears, and conduct in the light of revelation, particular circumstances of life, and personal dispositions, we discover over the course of time more and more of the truth about self and about who God calls us to be.

God talks back to us principally through the Word incarnate, Jesus Christ. We noted earlier in this chapter that Jesus is the answer we receive in prayer, even mystical prayer. If God speaks to us in revelation, as we just noted, that revelation is summed up and made concrete in Jesus. He speaks to us in the external circumstances of our lives and in our interior dispositions by their assuming meaning for us when examined in the light of what God says in Christ. For example, faced with the question of what to do when imposed upon by someone, I find an answer in Jesus' conduct in similar situations. If fearful of venturing on a ministry and wondering whether to undertake it or pass it by, the way Jesus handled similar fear enlightens me. Jesus' teaching more explicitly illuminates the meaning of my circumstances and my inner dispositions, though much thought and prayer may be required to see the precise application. Comparing ourselves to Jesus, we discover more about who we are, our strengths and weakness; in his true humanity we discern our own. From Jesus we also learn who we are called to be.

We learn that we are called to be the Father's very own unique son or daughter, beloved by him, brother or sister to the Son, guided and upheld by their Spirit. No one else understands us thoroughly. Some, perhaps our dearest friends, may even misunderstand us. We do not even understand ourselves! Forces are at work in the depths of our psyches to which we never penetrate, even with professional help. But through Jesus we know that the triune God understands us through and through, having created, redeemed, and sanctified us. They judge us justly—with no lack of understanding and no misunderstanding; they judge us compassionately, mercifully, forgivingly. They accept us completely, so much so that they invite us to share their intimate life with them for eternity.

To experience—not merely know in the head but feel in the heart—this mystery of the triune God's understanding, acceptance, and love for us is to have the true foundation of self-understanding, self-esteem, self-acceptance, and self-love which are necessary for healthy humanity and for generous love of others. While much understanding, esteem, acceptance, and love of self can be and often is generated by the understanding and love which people give us, what we derive from God in Jesus Christ through persevering practice of the prayer of presence is more basic, durable, and invigorating. It frees us to perceive and appreciate the imperfect, created understanding and love which people endeavor to give.

About ten years ago I was depressed because of a friendship which I finally realized was never going to be what I had hoped it would become. I was sitting in the chapel, praying, gazing at the huge crucifix over the altar. I do not recall the content of my prayer, but suddenly—like God's word sharper than any two-edged sword! (Heb. 4:12)—the thought penetrated me: He loves me even if no else ever does. Paul's words in Romans 5:8 came to mind: "It is precisely in this that God proves his love for us: that while we were still sinners, Christ died for us." In the prayer of presence the Father spoke to me his Word, Jesus, in answer to my need, and gave me a sense of self-worth that helps me to receive understanding and love from others, and to recover more easily and surely when deprived of that understanding and love.

If prayer is the expression to the Father, Son, and Holy Spirit of the stuff of daily life, then prayer is not limited to neat little packages of time set aside for it. We can be aware of the three divine Friends while walking down the street, taking a shower, or dropping off to sleep at night. During such times of solitude and of activities which do not engage the mind very much, we tend to rehearse in our minds personal plans for the future, disappointments of the past, pleasures previously enjoyed, and hostilities currently festering. These times are opportunities for prayer, for conversation with our three Friends about these matters. All that is required is recognition of being in their presence and the intention of directing our recital of woe or happiness to them for their help, so that we may bear the trial or appreciate the gift and thereby grow in love of them, ourselves, and our neighbor.

When we are engaged with people or with work or play, we will have, in the measure that friendship with the Father, Son, and Holy Spirit has taken hold of us, flashes of awareness of their presence and of our being about their business of loving men and women, serving them, and establishing God's reign in creation. I prefer to distinguish clearly between work, ministry, recreation, and prayer. One is not the other. Still all are expressions of friendship with the Father, Son, and Holy Spirit. They inspire and support each other and together actualize that friendship. Through all of them together we live for our Friends, and they become ever more real to us as Friends.

Times set aside for prayer, however, are still precious and zealously guarded. They are opportunities for more prolonged and full expression of thoughts and feelings to the three divine Persons. They are necessary for developing an inclination and facility for the prayer of presence, the goal of our efforts at prayer under the inspiration of grace. Times for prayer are simply refreshing moments with most loving Friends, flickering anticipations of eternal life in its fullness.

When setting times for prayer, we do well to consider first the rhythm of our lives, the pattern into which our work, our recreation, our meals, our rest fall. Then we can weave times for prayer into that rhythm—some times being scheduled in advance and habitually observed, other times being the result of sensing, so to speak, that life is now calling for an hour of prayer or for a day or two away in retreat. Times for prayer will be less trying, less distracted, if they form part of the rhythm of life; and the spirit of prayer will more easily flow into other activities or, better, other activities will flow more naturally from prayer, if the times for prayer are part of our distinctive pattern of life.

The rhythm of life, we should note, is not necessarily found within the span of twenty-four hours, a day. The cycle of activities which ordinarily make up our life is more likely to be found today in the period of a week, perhaps even a month for some people. It seems to have been an axiom of the past that if a prayer was worth engaging in, it should be undertaken every day. The resulting burden of prayers led to many of them becoming formalities or requiring extraordinary powers of concentration to make them authentic. The load of prayers to be fulfilled daily created tension with other necessary activities, to the profit of neither. We can quite possibly pray better, more intensely, less distractedly, if, for example, the amount of time given to mental prayer is greater on, let us say, Sunday than other days of the week, when many other duties are pressing; Monday to Friday we should perhaps be content with less lengthy times for the same prayer. A parish priest, on the other hand, will not likely find Sunday the best day for a long period of reflective prayer.

Communities, too, should consider the rhythm of community life in setting aside times for prayer. Here too a weekly rhythm of prayer may very often be the most realistic and the most fruitful in our day. Community prayer must be sufficient enough to express community and promote it; but it cannot be so consuming of time and energy that it prevents prayer by individuals according to the rhythm of their lives, especially the prayer of presence. On the other hand, community members in working out the place of prayer in the pattern of their individual lives, will need to incorporate community prayers as moments in their personal rhythm of life.

Communal prayer—liturgical, non-liturgical, formal,

spontaneous, charismatic—is valued at least because it contains the possibility that in some words or actions of the liturgy or a fellow Christian, a response of the Trinity to our prayer finally will be given to us: the Father, Son, and Holy Spirit will at last talk back! The dialogue between us and the Trinity will be consummated, and the freeing truth about ourselves and them will emerge into our consciousness.

The Father, Son, and Holy Spirit will not talk back every time we engage in common prayer, but certainly on some occasions a responding word will be there for us. Consequently, it is foolish to risk missing this word by neglect of such forms of prayer, or by too readily absenting ourselves on the grounds of not being in the mood. Our mood can change in the course of the prayer or, in spite of our mood, the word can still break through to us.

When this word from the Trinity does come to us in communal prayer, it continues to resound in mind and heart as we go our way, a new woman or a new man. We know self better and are more free, with greater potential for maturity. We are more intensely aware of the love bestowed upon us by our three divine Friends, now more vividly recognized as Friends.

In a previous paragraph we distinguished prayer from ministry, work, and recreation. We would distinguish it from anything else as well. Prayer's intrinsic purpose is raising the mind and heart to God in some way or another. Ministry's intrinsic purpose is providing for the needs of men and women. Work and anything else also have their respective intrinsic aims. So prayer is not to be confused with other activities. Nevertheless, prayer can accompany other activities, perhaps only in brief flashes lest one be distracted from the task at hand. The counselor must pay attention to what the counselee is saying: he or she cannot become absorbed in thoughts

about God's saving work in Jesus Christ or the significance of Christ's death on Calvary. Sometimes, however,
prayer can accompany other activities in a more enduring measure because the activities do not require so
much attention, like dusting a room or eating breakfast
alone.

Because prayer by its nature is attending to God, it is
the principal means of developing a sense of the Father,
Son, and Holy Spirit as Persons and Friends. It is also
the chief expression of friendship with them. Nevertheless, all our activities, viewed and motivated and offered
in prayer, become expressions of friendship with the
Trinity. We live, work, play for them and with them.
They are present as the horizon of our life's manifold
activities. As so present, they influence our choices at
least implicitly, or in a subconscious manner. We learn
to regard the Father, Son, and Holy Spirit as companions
at our side, assisting us as we go about our affairs—really
their affairs, for we see our activities as the realization
of their reign. Our activities are a divinely given participation in the Trinity's work of creation and sanctification. We are their friends whom they invite and em-
power to share in their activity. Thus we grow in our
sense of them—Father, Son, and Holy Spirit—as our
Friends.

As I write these lines, I am just a few miles from the
Golden Gate Bridge spanning the outlet of San Francisco
Bay into the Pacific Ocean. Two huge cables are anchored
on each side of the outlet and are slung across the waters
between two towers. The roadway is suspended from the
two giant cables by smaller vertical ones. The structure
of the roadway is designed to contribute as much support
as possible to its projection over the vast space between
shores, but the roadway still depends necessarily on the
mighty cables reaching from shore to shore. The roadway structure has broader surfaces than the cables and

receives the impact of wind and traffic. Because it is not rigidly fixed but suspended from the cables, however, it can move in the direction of the forces pounding upon it. Consequently, the impact of these forces is reduced and the roadway structure is less susceptible to damage from strong winds and heavy traffic. Winds, traffic, temperature affect the cables, of course; they are not immune to disturbance. They have, however, a strength and flexibility by which they can continue to be the principal support of the roadway even while undergoing stress themselves.

As the cables are the critical component of the Golden Gate Bridge, so friendship with the Father, Son, and Holy Spirit is the critical component of the celibate's life, as it is of every Christian's life. Everything else depends upon that friendship: self-esteem and self-confidence, human friendships, play, ministry, work for God's reign over creation. These other components have their own intrinsic values and strengths, but they still depend upon friendship with the Trinity. Indeed, because they are suspended, as it were, from that friendship, they can withstand better the forces which would often damage or destroy them. Self-esteem, interpersonal relationships, service of others, labor for God's kingdom may be battered by feelings of guilt or shame, by misunderstandings, conflicts, and failures; but they will not be totally destroyed and they will suffer less damage because upheld by friendship with the Father, Son, and Holy Spirit. Supported by the Trinity's faithful, forgiving love and by responsive faith, hope, and charity, life goes on with personal growth, human affection, ministry to others, and promotion of God's reign.

That supporting friendship with the Trinity is not, of course, immune to trials, any more than the cables of the bridge are immune to disturbance. Friendship with the Father, Son, and Holy Spirit entails the immense difficulties and sufferings peculiar to a relationship between a finite, fallible being and the infinite God. Moreover, personal psychological problems, floundering and flourishing friendships, frustrating and absorbing ministry, failures and successes in advancing God's reign can interfere with living in friendship with the Trinity or living in it intensely. But even in its own turmoil and when disturbed from without, that friendship with the triune God remains the principal strength and support of the whole of life. The effort to live it, both in its times of trial and in its times of tranquility, sustains everything else, whether that is going well or badly. Friendship with the Father, Son, and Holy Spirit supports everything else by giving it ultimate meaning and purpose, and often by improving what is going well or correcting what is going badly.

The adventure of celibate life includes growing in friendship not only with the Trinity but also with men and women. Therefore we now turn to human friendship in celibate life.

Chapter 7

AFFECTION IN CELIBATE LIFE

The expression **human friendship** has been used so far in a very general sense to cover various kinds of interpersonal relationships in a celibate's life. But we must be more precise now. We need to identify, describe, and appropriately name some of these relationships. The need for this clarification is not that we might have an accurate and complete classification of interpersonal relationships which a celibate may have, but that light may be thrown on affection in celibate life.

The full meaning of **affection** here will emerge as this chapter progresses. For the moment it suffices to say that the word is employed to designate our positive, warm, and even tender feelings, emotions, and acts of will in regard to persons. Its equivalent is the word **love** in its multiple analogous senses which enable us to use it in reference to many different levels and kinds of response to people; we speak, for example, of "loving" someone whose physical appearance pleases us, "loving" someone with whom we are infatuated, "loving" someone whose personality complements our own, or "loving" someone whom we serve because the person is in need. Affection has been preferred here to designate the range of our positive reactions to people because it is less burdened with connotations of physical attraction and highly charged emotions than love often is.

Affection in celibate life deserves attention because its presence is questioned. The celibate awakens in people's minds not simply the question why he or she is celibate, but the question what his or her life can possibly be like. If a person excludes from life love between man and woman and consequently love between parents and children, what can be left of affection in his or her life? Will he ever enjoy the subtle pleasure of another's hand resting in his, or she the satisfaction of another's arms wrapped around her? Will he ever feel his heart leap with delight at the unexpected appearance of someone, or she feel thrilled by someone's attention? Will she ever experience security, or he confidence, arising from admiring eyes? Will she ever enjoy the softness of an infant in her arms, or sense her value as she bandages the scraped knee of a child? Will he ever sense his power as he playfully tussles on the floor with a baby? When he walks alone in solitude or in a crowd, will he feel comfort in the awareness that he is at the center of someone else's life? Will he or she ever feel accomplishment at the sight of a son's or daughter's graduation, marriage, or ordination?

These instances of affection and countless others that could be mentioned are each small, transient, and taken for granted; nobody would die for any single one of them. Yet all together they constitute a large portion of human life which human nature cries out for and drives toward. If all such affection is ruled out of celibate life, can that life be anything but cold, arid, and lonely? Can satisfying food, clothing, shelter, work to be done, and even a cause to struggle for compensate for the absence of affection?

The fact is that affection is not foreign to celibate life. In this chapter I intend to reflect on some experiences of affection in my celibate life to suggest the variety of affection which celibates can enjoy.

Difficult to isolate and put into words is affection felt

for and from my religious community. By **community** here I mean the local community and I mean that community, not in the sense of an organization, a legally constituted entity, but in the sense of men with whom I live, pray, work, and play daily—companions in living and in pursuing the ideal of St. Dominic. Though the membership of this community changes regularly, some men remain in it many years, most for several years, so that we have an opportunity to become at least familiar with each other and, in some instances, close.

But community here means more than the group of men with whom I live daily. It includes the life which we live together. That life together is an important constitutive of community. Indeed, community is not constituted simply by many people happening to be in the same place a good part of their time, but by their sharing in the pursuit of some goal. By my local religious community, then, I do not mean simply a "nice bunch of guys" who happen to reside and work and recreate where I do, but men engaged with one another in activities conducive to human, Christian, and Dominican goals.

This community exists because its members strive for community as much as because they have it. In other words, one of the goals which binds people in community is the pursuit of community. It will be otherwise in the world to come, perhaps. Certainly in this world community is not just "there" for us to look at and then decide whether or not to join it. Only in joining with others in the making of community can one find community. Community consists, moreover, in continuously making community. So the local religious community to which I am referring is not a romantic ideal. Composed of ordinary men, it has its flaws, weaknesses, and troubled moments, as well as its beautiful features.

The community of which I write is large, ranging between forty to sixty men from year to year. Ten years ago and more, it went even beyond that number. As a community staffing a school of theology and as a community of formation, it has a relatively permanent core of twenty to twenty-five men. My relationship to individual members has ranged from superficial to intimate. But my belonging to the community embraces not simply my relationships to its individuals taken one by one, but also my participation in the life which all those individuals live together. That life I highly value. Since each member contributes to it, he is important to me, though perhaps on a one-to-one basis we have not shared extensively with each other. I am not recommending this situation but reporting it as a fact—a fact which does not preclude feeling affection for and from this community or, more precisely, for and from the men actively engaged in continuously making this community.

The community is, in my judgment, a good community. Members have generally striven over the years to be open and honest with each other, to dialogue over issues, to plan life together, and to cooperate in living it. We have grown in all these activities over the years. As in all growth, we have experienced not only progress but also stalemate and even reversal. Tensions, divisions, and even confrontations there have been. But we have worked through them and experienced moments of extraordinary brotherhood. We will continue to encounter difficulties; we have not arrived in the heavenly Jerusalem. But we can have confidence about the future because of the past.

I love this community and feel its love for me. Or more precisely, I love these men in our life together, and I feel their love for me and my having a place in their life. It is a subtle sort of love or affection, difficult to describe except by talking around it.

I miss these people and our life together when I am away. I miss the community, not in the sense of being "broken up" because separated from it, but in the sense of being aware that I am not surrounded by what is familiar and comfortable. I cherish this community as the origin of much of what I am wherever I may be. It provides a sense of security wherever I may be, and it supports my freedom to be who I am, anywhere. It serves me as a model for what to strive after in any group with which I become associated. I desire to return to this community when away.

When I leave the community or when it disperses for work or vacation, I feel a tinge of sadness. I feel disappointment when someone leaves the community for another ministry and hence life in another community. Returning to the community after being away, or experiencing the community gathering again after dispersal, feels like getting into an old pair of slippers at the end of a busy day. I feel pleasure when a new member comes to share the life we have.

When at home, that is, abiding in the community, I experience many feelings of affection. Basic is the feeling of belonging, of being a part of a group and a part of other people's lives through and in our common life. I feel welcomed, esteemed, appreciated. When in a community meeting we deliberate some aspect of our life, I feel support for my own striving after the objectives we all share, even if my particular interpretation of those objectives differs. When we meet to review our income, expenditures, and budget, I feel responsibility to others, and others care for my needs and even wishes. In fact, I have been especially impressed at others' concern that I have what I feel I need in the way of educational, professional, and living expenses. The warmth of brotherhood is strongly felt when together we have a special meal, go for a picnic, sit around a fire on a winter's evening, or celebrate a liturgy of profession or ordination.

It can be objected that what has been described is good but it falls short of the intensity and intimacy of affection that is found in relationships with one other person or with only a few. In answer it should be noted, first, that the sort of affection described so far is crucial for life, fulfilling a very basic need which everyone has, and hence ought not to be undervalued. This sort of affection is what makes life generally bearable and satisfying. It is perhaps not the peak experience of affection, but it provides a milieu for peak experiences and readies individuals for them in the community or outside of it.

Secondly, the community of which I speak is lovable and comforting precisely because it contains the potential for intense and intimate affection on a one-to-one basis. We often fail to find community because we hold back from engaging with others to make community. Likewise we fail to experience affection more intensely and intimately in a community because we hesitate to share our deeper selves with individual members of the community. But more than once in my life when I was grievously troubled, or overawed by some happening, or especially happy, I have shared these feelings with one or another member of the community in which I was living at the time—a member with whom I had previously shared only more general fellowship. I have always found readiness to receive what I had to say sympathetic response and willingness on the part of the brother to share more of himself with me.

From these experiences the conviction has been born in me that within my community lies a depth of affection which is far beyond what normally appears and which is ready to surface whenever I need it—perhaps not from everyone but from nearly all. Out of that conviction is born a feeling of security and worth akin, I suspect, to what a wife or husband feels vis-à-vis his or her partner. There is someone to turn to! If this intense and intimate affection does not come to the surface so very frequently, that is not because the affection is not there, but because it is not tapped for reasons usually of my own making: I am too busy; I presume I am imposing; I still let fears impede revealing my inmost self to others.

The affection which I feel between myself and the members of my religious community is a blend of what C. S. Lewis in his book **The Four Loves** names affection (note the narrower sense of the word in Lewis's usage), companionship, and friendship.[1] Affection (in Lewis's sense) is the comfortable, at-home feeling we enjoy with familiar people in whose presence we do not need to be so much on guard as to how we present ourselves, for we are already well known. If we become angry occasionally, we do not have to fear not being invited back. Others will understand, bear with us until our anger blows over, and take up with us again when we have cooled down. Companionship, in distinction from affection, is the feeling of unity arising from our cooperation with one another in various projects, above all the effort to create a Christian Dominican community with its peculiar inner life and overflowing ministry. Friendship, as distinct from affection and companionship, is the feeling of oneness derived from our sharing a similar vision of Christian life and ministry: all of us have been attracted by the ideal of St. Dominic as the way to realize Christian life and ministry.

The feelings of affection. companionship, and friendship between me and each member of the community vary. of course. in proportion to several factors. for example, the length of time we have been together, the number and kind of projects we have worked at together, or perhaps the interpretation we have of the ideal of St. Dominic. But when all these feelings between myself

1—(New York: Harcourt. Brace. and World. 1960), pp. 53-127.

and individuals, and me and the community as a whole,
are added together, it is evident that affection (in our
sense, not Lewis's) is a large part of my celibate life.

The immensity of this affection has led me to a view
of the vows quite different from the view I had when I
first thought of religious life and during my earlier years
as a religious. Then I conceived the vows—not simply
the ceremonial profession but the living of them—as
making me very independent. Poverty, religious chastity, and obedience would free me from material things,
people, and myself. I would be free as the wind to go
anywhere, live with anybody, and do whatever had to be
done for the sake of the kingdom. Life has taught me my
limitations.

Among these limitations is my need, not to be free of
people, but to be related to them—and deeply related to
some. My vows make me dependent more than independent. By my vows I insert my life into the lives of
others, humbly acknowledging my need for their affection and assistance, and recognizing that my service of
God consists radically in giving my limited self to others
for their welfare. My poverty is not freedom from material things as much as my dependence on others for
the necessities of life and ministry. My religious chastity
is not freedom from people but dependence on them for
the affection and help I need to grow in self-knowledge
and self-esteem, so that I can love others. My obedience
is not freedom from the needs of my humanity and my
peculiar personality but dependence on others for their
acceptance of my needs. Such acceptance will allow and
enable me to fulfill these needs. My obedience is also
dependence on others for their assistance in putting my
talents to good use for the sake of God's reign.

Detachment, then, is not so much being free of things,
people, and self. It is not being "above" these. It is much
more the willingness and readiness to shift dependence

on others from one material situation of life and ministry to another, from the affection and help of one group of people to those of another group, from one form of others' acceptance and assistance to another form. Detachment is not wresting self free of human nature, individual personality, and affection received and given. That is simply impossible. Striving for it is chasing wind. Detachment entails humbly accepting humanity and personality with their needs; it involves being willing and ready to relinquish dependence on one group of people for life's needs and to grow in dependnce on another group.

Detachment is difficult and painful because it involves not only leaving one satisfying and edifying ambience of affection but also entering into another one. As a result of the pain involved in separation from those whom we have loved and depended upon, we may decide never again to become dependent on others or to allow affection between ourselves and others. But the former decision is impossible to carry out except in our own minds, and the latter decision is cowardly and ultimately self-destructive. Neither decision is truly detachment but unrecognized selfishness or illusory sanctity.

Within the ambit of my religious community, two other experiences of affection have been significant in my life. The first was the feeling of being welcomed, valued, and enjoyed by several members of the community some fifteen to twenty years older than I. This experience occurred in the year prior to and following my ordination to the priesthood. These men seem to have taken a liking to the group of us who were at the same stage in our religious life. They hosted us for outdoor barbecues in the park. They shared with us together and individually their experiences and views. They showed interest in our work, our growth, our plans for the future. I shall never forget the warmth these men provided in my life during those years, and I shall always be grateful to them for this affection for me and my brothers—an affection which awoke in me special affection for them.

The second significant experience of affection rather surprised me when I became aware of it. I had now become an "older" member of the community. I became conscious of some younger men's respect, admiration, and affection for me. It was startling to realize that I was being loved by young people. Perhaps for the first time I was explicitly conscious of the fulfilling feeling of being accepted, esteemed, loved. I had been the recipient of much affection throughout my life, but previously I had not known how crucial it is for personal development and had not been reflectively aware that I was being given so precious a gift. Emotionally it was like being hoisted on shoulders and carried through a cheering crowd. A reciprocal affection grew in me or, more accurately I suspect, awareness of a reciprocal affection. I saw more clearly and valued more consciously the particular personalities and talents of these men.

Out of this experience was born an abiding appreciation for the young members of my community. I value their contribution to my life. They raise year after year the fundamental questions, so that I have to answer them afresh for myself as well as for them. They compel me to recognize that other visions and values than mine are born of different environments and times. They remind me that life is struggling to discover and fulfill a vision. In a word, they keep me intellectually and spiritually alive and open. I do not find it easy to have to do battle once again over issues already debated more than once. I can be annoyed at having my values and familiar way of life questioned. But I know that in the long run these disturbances are good for me.

To note the growth of these younger members of the

community from their uncertain first months in our midst is a source of admiration, joy, and satisfaction to me. My feelings may not be exactly the same as those of a father watching his own children grow from infancy through childhood, but the similarity of feelings is obvious. Likewise, I experience moments of quiet pride when I witness one of these young men preach a particularly profound homily, preside over a Eucharist with special effectiveness, or perform in some other way with competence. My feeling is a combination of joy for them in their achievement, wonder at the development which has led to this moment, satisfaction at having contributed to it, and happiness in seeing values which I have cherished now being realized in another generation.

C. S. Lewis in **The Four Loves** remarks that friendship in the ancient understanding of it—Aristotle's **philia** and Cicero's **amicitia**—is rarely understood and experienced in modern society. We tend to call friends those who are acquaintances, companions, familiars, or lovers. We ourselves have been using the term friendship in a broad sense to cover many different kinds of relationships. But among my experiences of affection I can single out one kind that matches the description of friendship in the strict sense in which C. S. Lewis uses the word.

In my early twenties, before I became a Dominican, I spent many hours over a year or two with a fellow student. We enjoyed talking about philosophy, theology, literature, and the arts. Our ways parted but without trauma. We did not correspond. though through mutual acquaintances we usually had at least a vague idea of what each was doing. Approximately a dozen years later, when for several months I was in the same city as he, we arranged to spend a day together. When we met, our conversation picked up as if our last meeting had been the day before rather than a decade before. Amazing was not the fact of ready conversation, for we had plenty of information to exchange after more than ten years apart, but the feeling that accompanied the conversation. That feeling was one of familiarity but more significantly one of "being on the same wave length," of "being in tune," of having the same interests, the same general values, even though we had very different opinions about specific things, for example, certain changes in the Church and political approaches to social problems. Subsequent get-togethers during the months we were in the same city were always especially comfortable times.

This experience illustrates clearly the unique character of friendship in the stricter sense of the term as used by C. S. Lewis.[2] It is an affection based, not on bodily or emotional need or attraction, but on shared vision and values. We live, work, play, and pray with others. When we talk about what we do together, we perhaps discover someone in the group who has questions very similar to ours, or who interprets or evaluates the shared activities in much the same way we do. When we speak in the midst of our associates in a common project, we sense that one or another truly understands what we are saying. We have an affinity with him or her that we do not feel with others who share the same activities and the same discussion of them. If we have problems about what is going on in life—life in general which we share with every human being, or a particular sphere of life which we share with some—we go to that person who, as we have discovered in general conversation, sees and feels about life as we do, and he or she can sympathize with us, grasp the import of our questions, and offer answers which make sense to us.

2—The next several paragraphs are much indebted to Lewis's *The Four Loves*, pp. 87-111.

The gift quality of this kind of affection is prominent. It is not continually flowing out of some biological or psychic spring only looking for someone to attach itself to. As individuals we can survive without it and so too can the human race. It is not offered to us as frequently as attraction to a beautiful face, a strong personality, a genial companion. We never find it by looking for it, because it appears only when we are attending to something else. Friendship happens, not because two people see each other, but because they see the same third thing.

Of course, once two people discover their shared vision and values, they begin to notice each other more closely; then other kinds of affection may arise. Likewise, other kinds of affection may bring two people together in activities and conversation, and then they discover friendship. Marriage counselors sometimes say that the lovers who enter marriage must become friends if their marriage is to survive. Physical and emotional attraction to one another is not enduring enough, or at least not stable enough, to sustain marriage. Once the affection of friendship is discovered, it can be cultivated by continual sharing of activities and conversation. Friendship develops through joint experiences in many areas of life and the exploration of the meaning and value of those experiences.

Because it is not fulfilling a basic biological or psychic need for survival or sanity, the affection of friendship does not wax and wane on the basis of our metabolism and moods. In fact, this sort of affection better than any other enables us to endure the ups and downs of life and of other kinds of affection. Because a friend's affection for us is not entangled in her or his own emotions relative to us, she or he is free to notice our emotional or physical suffering, to help us look objectively at a problem, and to act for our welfare when we are prevented by illness or injury, depression or grief. Precisely as friend, we, in turn, are free to support and provide for others in significant ways.

Of course there are many degrees of friendship in the narrow sense depending upon the extent of common understanding and values; and friendship is associated with other kinds of affection which promote or prevent it. Looking back over my celibate life, I find in it many instances of the affection of friendship in many different degrees and in various combinations. The affection of friendship is an element in my general affection for my religious community and its members, as noted above. I have experienced the affection of friendship with particular individuals all along the course of my life, both with members of my religious community and outsiders, with women as well as men.

Once again we see that celibate life is not void of affection. In the case of friendship in the strict sense, however, we ought to note the modern tendency which C. S. Lewis points out: we generally miss the experience of this sort of affection. Ever since the Romantic movement, Lewis observes, the affection of friendship has been too anemic for us; it is not sentimental or passionate enough. In an age which thinks of men and women as products of evolution, it does not have enough of the animal in it and is of no value for survival; indeed it threatens a group. It also violates romantic ideals of democracy and equality.

Celibates, hungry for affection like other human beings, have a special need to discern, appreciate, and cultivate friendship in the narrow sense. I do not say this because this sort of affection is very compatible with religious chastity and therefore safe to admit into one's life, although this is true. I say it because this affection of friendship is indeed supporting and enriching and makes life beautiful; and celibate life is usually lived in contexts which are fertile soil for such affection. To be-come conscious of, esteem, and develop the affection of friendship is simply to cultivate and reap a harvest of affection which celibate life offers a person. In writing these pages I have reflected as never before on this kind of affection in the course of my celibate life. I have only now seen how supporting, comforting, and inspiring it has been in the long run. Because of its spiritual qualities and its freedom from organic and psychic needs, how-ever, I feel that I have insufficiently appreciated it.

Another experience of affection in my life has been that which I have felt for individuals or groups whom I have served as teacher, counselor, retreat director, or celebrant of the Eucharist. In serving these people, I was aware of a satisfaction which came, not simply from the work I was doing for them, but from the relationship to them. I experienced myself attracted to them, feeling positively about them, enjoying them, wishing that our relationship was not limited to the service being given and its brief span of time. I have been impressed over the years by teachers, grade and high school, who have affirmed with obvious earnestness their affection for the children or young people whom they taught. Their satis-faction derived less from the work or ministry they were performing than from the people to whom they were related in that ministry.

It has taken me time to know what to do with this affection. Some of the advice I heard in my youth was to ignore these feelings. They were dangerous because they were feelings of affection and hence constituted an attachment opposed to the ideal of Christian holiness. Or though good in themselves, they would interfere with effective ministry because affection would prevent me from being objective and others from revealing their problems. Besides, letting affection for some people take its natural course would lead to conduct indicative of preferences and even partiality, so that effectiveness in regard to others would be prevented. Friendship and ministry are best kept apart; let them flourish but independently of each other.

Today I would qualify the elements of this advice. The feelings of affection could be dangerous but are not necessarily so; and if dangerous, for other reasons than those perhaps usually implied. The idea that affection can interfere with the expression of problems and with objective response to them is true sometimes and then in varying degrees, but is not true always and in every regard. On the contrary, affection with its concomitant trust can facilitate self-revelation, and with its sympathy it can improve perception. Mature love promotes objectivity. Affection manifested for one or some may deter others from seeking my service, but it need not do so. If it does, then the question is whether the problem is mine or theirs. I need to keep in mind that I have personal needs to be met and that I cannot normally expect to serve everyone. It is necessary to weigh carefully in every situation how much friendship with some is going to hinder ministry to many.

Keeping ministry and friendship separate realms is a handy, safe rule which forestalls having to make many particular decisions and perhaps occasionally judging wrongly. On the other hand, the rule risks depersonalizing ministry and missing a rich realm of affection in celibate life.

Eugene Kennedy, in his book **Comfort My People,** emphasizes that the priest or religious ministers to others through his or her person.[3] Ministry is not an impersonal function of transferring a quantity of grace from God to a recipient, but a person's being for another the vehicle of God's transforming action which is a personal invitation

---

3—(New York: Sheed and Ward, 1968), pp. 29-39.

calling for a personal response. The whole person, not only skills of ministry and external activity, is involved to some degree in serving another, if the service is according to the pattern of Jesus, who is God-as-man encountering men and women. Affection for those served and affection from them are legitimately acknowledged and accepted as integral to ministry.

This acknowledgment and acceptance are important for celibates. To ignore or deny this affection is not only to venture on the risky path of suppressing or repressing feelings rather than dealing with them; it is also to deprive self of a wealth of affection, given and received, generally supportive of life and enriching it. Sometimes this affection can be crucially necessary. A celibate may be in a situation—for example, long hours of ministering in an isolated apostolate—wherein the principal human affection sustaining daily life is that which is found in the relationships arising in his or her ministry. In this case, to ignore or deny the affection discovered in ministering to people could be to drive self needlessly into a desert of loneliness in which survival becomes very difficult. To acknowledge, enjoy, and draw refreshment from the affection for and from others encountered in ministry is simply to accept a gift of God, his love in human form.

The affection we are speaking about here is, of course, mature and judiciously expressed. The advice about keeping ministry and friendship separate has not arisen without grounds. Immature, neurotic, or inferior sorts of affection in us or in those to whom we minister can interfere with ministry. We need to remember, also, that we do not always know the true quality of the affection which we feel towards others and which others feel towards us. Affection can even lead us to deceive ourselves. So we must proceed carefully in mingling friendship and ministry. But the fact remains which we wish to emphasize here, namely, that affection has a place in ministering and hence in celibate life.

The place which many kinds of affection have in celibate life is not begrudgingly granted, so to speak. It is not as if affection is there as a matter of fact but not by right, or as if affection is there because celibacy is usually imperfect. Celibacy is a way of being human. Hence it provides a place for many kinds of love. If the celibate is denying or suppressing those various kinds of affection for people in his or her life, he or she is very likely smothering affection in prayer, making it more trying and less satisfying.

Celibacy is meant to promote that selfless love of God and neighbor which the New Testament calls **agape** (or **caritas** in Latin and **charity** in English). This purpose of celibacy does not mean that celibacy leads to the exclusion of the many kinds of human affection in order to replace them by **agape**. Grace perfects nature; grace does not destroy it. Christian love of God and neighbor, which the Holy Spirit inspires and we seek, permeates various kinds of human love, manifests itself through them, and in the process tempers, harmonizes, and integrates them into a life lived unto God for fellow human beings. These loves, on their part, promote the intensity of **agape** by providing additional motives for loving God and neighbor. The uniqueness of agape and its vigor are manifested in doing good to enemies and to people for whom we have no affection; but its vehemence and joy are revealed in doing good to people loved humanly in various ways.

To assert the compatibility of celibacy, agape, and affection of many kinds is not to claim that we do not have to struggle to achieve the purity of each and the harmony of all. Given the human condition, effort—often painful effort— is inevitable in our striving for authentic celibacy, charity, affection, and the balance of all three.

Approximating that goal (we never fully attain it) becomes especially challenging when the relationship between two people includes strong emotional involvement and physical attraction. Such involvement and attraction are prominent ingredients of what popularly goes by the name **love.** In the following chapters we will be considering this kind of love between men and women in celibate life. The principles guiding the interpretation and handling of that love apply to love between celibates of the same sex.

Chapter 8

HUMAN LOVE AND PRAYER

Some men and women pledged to religious celibacy fall in love with one another. They have in the past, they do today, and very likely will do so in the future. They may develop a deep love unwittingly as the result of long association in work. They may discover a strong bond of love as a not clearly foreseen result of cultivating an initial attraction whose nature they did not fully apprehend in the beginning. Whatever way the experience occurs, when it is recognized religious celibates are faced with the question of what to do about it.

Some will advise that the kind of love between man and woman which usually leads to marriage is simply incompatible with religious celibacy. One should be alert to resist even the first stirrings of such love. Once its existence is recognized, it should be rejected and the relationship generating and sustaining it cleanly broken. Others will say that if the love is genuine, it is a sign that the couple are not meant to be celibate. Their celibate commitments should be set aside in favor of marriage; the latter is clearly their vocation.

Both of these answers are unsatisfactory. Even if the first answer were theoretically correct, it is not practical. It is a message which those experiencing the exhilaration of human love are not disposed to hear, much less accept. Paradoxically, that answer is tantamount to recommending that they give up their dedication to celibate life. The value of human love at this point appears obvious and immediately satisfying, while the value of celibacy can be perceived only in the obscurity of faith and grasped in an unknown future. If a choice has to be made, it will very probably be for marriage. Rather than advice simply to "stop it," guidance is needed about what to do with all the feelings and how to express them, so that a point of tranquillity and clear-sightedness can be reached. Then a decision can be made where celibacy will have a chance of winning out.

The second answer is wasteful of celibacy, abandoning it all too readily. It too easily deprives both Church and society of valuable witness and service, and the couple of possibly beautiful lives including mutual celibate love. Attractive and talented men and women who could easily have won spouses and yet chose not to for the sake of God's kingdom do confound the secularist mentality and jolt people into questioning the purpose of life. Many services are rendered to underprivileged or suffering people by religious celibates who fill their lives with concern for these people. The possibility of celibate love is not so obvious, but the lives of some saints provide models of what might be.

Both answers have common faults. Each in a different way is unappreciative of human love's potentialities on the one hand and, on the other, religious celibacy's. The first answer does not perceive the power of human love to intensify celibate dedication; two people can love one another into religious dedication, including celibacy. The first answer conceives of celibacy more in terms of opposition to human love than in terms of a manner of loving humanly. The second answer underestimates the power of human love to flourish with a modicum of physical presence and expression. It fails to see the power of celibate dedication to confirm and enrich human love.

In both answers the expectations of human love between man and woman are tainted by the standards of a sensate, sex-saturated culture rather than derived from ideals of personal dignity and genuine love. Both answers presume that if a man and woman love one another, they must go to bed together, in marriage or outside of it. Yet millions of men and women go to bed together without any love for one another.

Love is popularly understood all too often as mutual physical attraction and genital satisfaction. But physical human love and gives it a certain fulfillment but is not its essence. According to Harry Stack Sullivan, "when the satisfaction or the security of another person becomes attraction is only an invitation to discover a person whom one may then love. Mutual genital pleasure expresses as significant to one as one's own satisfaction or security, then the state of love exists."[1] Rollo May defines love as "a delight in the presence of the other person and an affirming of his value and development as much as one's own."[2] Neither definition necessarily requires genital sexual pleasure for its fulfillment.

Another answer is proposed these days—the so-called third way. There are different understandings of the third way. It certainly means a close relationship, involving physical sex, between a man and a woman, at least one of whom is bound to celibacy. Some include in the third way even a close relationship between such people without physical sex. This latter relationship should not be included, for such a relationship can still be in the

---

1—*Conceptions of Modern Psychiatry* (2nd ed.; New York: W. W. Norton and Co., 1961, c1953), pp. 42-43.

2—*Man's Search for Himself* (New York: W. W. Norton and Co., 1953), p. 241.

way of authentic religious celibacy. Not a few men and women saints appear to have had close relationships, yet no one has claimed that they were following a third way.

The third way, too, is an unsatisfactory answer. It entails some kind of deception, either pretending to be celibate or allowing others to think so, when one is not even trying to be. For the sake of argument, we may even grant that possibly the third way does not violate the interior inspiration of one's commitment; it is conceivable that one may honestly decide before God that he does not expect one's commitment to remain binding because of major changes in the conditions of one's life. But the third way does violate the public aspect of the commitment, for release from the public commitment is not sought. We may also question the genuineness of a love which does not respect one's own or another's past public commitment which partially constitutes who a person is in the present.

A fourth possible answer is that celibate dedication and human love are not necessarily incompatible and can be mutually enriching if harmonized; but since they are difficult to reconcile in practice, the experience of human love is, therefore, a problem for religious celibates.

The premise of this answer is balanced. It respects the nature, values, and potentialities of both religious celibacy and human love, but acknowledges that the coincidence of the two is not easily handled. Each has its own tendencies and demands which conflict with the other's at certain points. Tensions and frustrations inevitably result from the attempt to combine the two. Harmonizing these divergent tendencies, balancing these conflicting demands, resolving the resultant tensions constitute a formidable challenge.

The conclusion of this answer, however, is questionable. Is it right to say that human love is a problem for religious celibates? Is it right to reduce human love to a problem, even for celibates? Ought it not be regarded as a gift and a mystery? Its occurrence may create problems, but it is not itself a problem, but an awesome gift.

One of people's deepest needs is for various kinds of love given and received: between parents and children, between peers and friends, between men and women. Millions of human beings suffer from the lack of various kinds of love. Countless personality problems are traceable to a lack of love. But genuine love cannot be bought or bargained for. It cannot be generated for another or evoked for one's self merely by willing it. True, we can and must work to provide the conditions for its occurrence, survival, and growth. But its advent, duration, and development are not directly the product of conscious efforts. We are aware that our various loves, both bestowed and received, are given to us, often in spite of ourselves. They possess us rather than we possess them. Even for celibates, the initial reaction to potentially wholesome love of any kind ought not to be perplexity before a problem but gratitude for a gift.

Human love between man and woman is a mystery to be admired, revered, explored, and treasured, not a problem to be analyzed, attacked, solved, and set aside. In keeping with the modern penchant for subjecting more and more areas of environment and life to technique, psychology and psychiatry are prone to treat love as a problem. The endeavor serves worthy purposes but only complements and does not replace the poet's or philosopher's vision. Martin Heidegger and Gabriel Marcel have warned of the dire consequences deriving from humanity's forgetfulness of being and its mystery, which must be contemplated and enjoyed rather than reduced to technical problems and utilized.

Human love cures depressing anxiety, begets self-confidence, heightens perception, magnifies sensitiveness, facilitates compassion, inspires enthusiasm for life, pro-

vides a sense of well-being and fulfillment which manifest themselves in the eyes, the face, the step of a woman
or a man. Perhaps humanly devised techniques can produce comparable results, but not at the depth of personal
being and with the deftness of love. The power of love
to transform personality, vision, and life is awesome.
In the presence of such power we are provoked to wonder about it and to respect its force. Our appetite is
whetted to taste more of its marvels. To set it aside
seems equivalent to foregoing life itself. No wonder the
author of The First Letter of John (4:8) wrote that God
is love!

We can compare human love to faith in Jesus Christ.
Such faith is a gift. One cannot reason one's self into it
or be argued by another into it. One cannot simply will
its existence in one's life. Steps may be taken to open
one's self or another to the possibility of believing in
Christ, but sincerely saying "I believe" is a gift: "No one
can say: 'Jesus is Lord,' except in the Holy Spirit" (I Cor.
12:3). Indeed, even taking the steps to open one's self to
the possibility of faith is ultimately a gift.

This faith is also a mystery. Its origin is a source of
wonder. Its firmness in spite of the inconclusiveness of
its rational foundations is always an enigma. Its power
to transform life is amazing: it bears in its womb the most
intimate communion with God, the richest of mystical
experience, and the fullest apostolic service, as Jean
Mouroux so beautifully shows in his book **I Believe.**

To reduce faith to a problem rather than see it as a
precious gift and fathomless mystery is foolish. But
without question its advent in one's life raises problems.
It calls for hard choices between, on the one hand, attitudes and actions which are consonant with it and, on
the other, positions and conduct which follow purely
human and often sinful standards. Similarly, human love
is not a problem even though it raises problems.

But is not human love sometimes a curse rather than a gift? Can it not be demonic, inspiring fear and flight rather than admiration and reverence? Does it not often ravage and even destroy human lives? Is not this destructiveness the theme of numerous dramas, novels, and operas?

A first answer is yes, but that response still does not make human love simply a problem subject to technical reason's manipulation. It only deepens the mystery of love, acknowledging a dark, destructive side of it. Or it may be that human love may appear to be a curse and demonic, not because it is such in itself, but because of the frailty of the human egos upon which it has its impact. We consider faith in Jesus Christ as a gift and mystery, but it has sometimes resulted in fanaticism, devastating the lives of countless others and proving to be a curse for its possessors. This demonic and damning quality of fanatical faith in Christ we would not attribute to that faith itself, but to the weakness of personality which often fails to handle well the greatest gifts of life.

The human love which religious celibates experience can be understood, then, in various ways. We would be mistaken not to take seriously the challenge which it presents to celibacy, the limitations which it must endure under celibacy, the tensions, conflicts, and problems which result from it in celibate life, and the unfortunate consequences which can issue from its occurrence. But we would also be mistaken not to esteem it as a wonderful gift and a beautiful mystery, even though not every celibate experiences it or must experience it for personal fulfillment.

The wonder of this gift and the beauty of this mystery are, in part, that it can nourish prayer, intensify love of God and neighbor, and inspire more intelligent and firm celibate commitment. In the mature celibate seriously dedicated to her or his vocation, human love not only can but will lead to these results. Intensified prayer, deeper union with God, increased love of neighbor, and stronger celibate dedication in turn enable the celibate to refine the human love and assimilate it into her or his religious life for that life's enrichment.

The celibate's experience of human love begets pleasure, satisfaction, joy, and a zest for life. Deep cisterns of human and personal needs are filled to brimming with cool, fresh water. Life becomes extraordinarily beautiful in the present and rich in possibilities for the future. The celibate admires the qualities discovered, one after the other, in the loved one and marvels at the total uniqueness and mystery of the beloved's being. In the beloved's presence, life assumes a timeless, eternal quality. Particular words and actions are lost to view in the more comprehensive awareness of the interpersonal presence which they mediate; just being together is more significant than anything said or done. Because of this affective bond, the whole of life and the world receive a new interpretation and meaning.

A frequent form of prayer found in the Bible is praise of God in thanksgiving for his gifts of creation and salvation. The Bible contains countless joyful songs (psalms and canticles) in which God is praised and thanked simply by recalling in his presence the beauty and awesomeness of creation and his wonderful works of salvation on behalf of his people or individuals. In the pleasure, satisfaction, and joy which the celibate finds in his or her human love, there is inspiration for praise of God and thanksgiving to him for what gives so much happy fulfillment.

As the wonderfulness of both the experience and the loved one is rehearsed in mind—one can scarcely avoid doing this—the celibate has only to place self in the presence of God and add to the rehearsal, in a spirit of gratitude, acknowledgment to God for his gift. Knowing experientially what it means to break out in praise and thanksgiving to God for one gift so keenly appreciated, the celibate more readily values the liturgy, which consists largely of prayers of praise and thanksgiving for other gifts of God, many of them far more important than this human love. Periods of mental prayer are welcomed, for they provide time to recount before God, in thankful praise, the joys of the love experienced.

But there is also the pain of separation—the anguish of parting and the ache of being apart. What is to be done with this pain? It is united with the pain which Christ once suffered on the cross and thus it is made, not an inexplicable dead-end, but a way toward life, discerned in the mystery of Jesus' resurrection. The celibate unites his or her pain with that of Christ whenever the pain is felt with particular acuteness, but also when he or she offers self to God in, with, and through Christ in the celebration of the Eucharist. The pain of separation is grist for the mill of union with Christ in suffering and death, even as the joy of presence anticipates the joy of sharing in the resurrection of Jesus. Through the pains and joys of love, the celibate shares in the paschal mystery of Christ. Grateful consciousness of this fact in the presence of God is a simple form of prayer.

To alleviate the ache of being apart from the loved one, the celibate will spontaneously recall times of being together and will look forward in anticipation to future meetings. Here too is the stuff of prayer. Liturgical prayer is, among other things, memorial. It is remembrance of God's saving action when he has been especially present to his people, particularly in Jesus Christ, revealing his love, his purpose, his power, and even his inner life as Father, Son, and Holy Spirit. Liturgical prayer also looks to the future. The liturgical season of Advent, Christmas, and Epiphany, for example, in recalling

Christ's first coming, looks forward to his future return in glory when God's reign will be definitively established, the dead will rise, and heaven and earth will be finally renewed. The celibate can convert into prayer both recollection of past times with the beloved and anticipation of future encounters by making memories of the past the occasion for praise and thanksgiving to God, and by making dreams of the future the occasion for petition and expressions of hope for the fulfillment of God's will.

The pleasure or comfortableness experienced in the presence of the loved one, the pain felt in separation, and the constant drift of thoughts toward the beloved make the celibate aware that in this relationship celibacy is powerfully challenged. The choice of celibacy bestowed the freedom to love many, and here is an invitation to realize that love in part. But response to this particular invitation is especially challenging because the celibate is attracted to someone who fulfills his or her needs for sexual complementarity at every level, including the desire for genital sex. These needs are very profound and the desire is perhaps very strong. Attraction to someone who is perceived as satisfying them is very, very powerful. For the first time, or anew, the celibate sees with special clarity how great a good has been set aside in choosing to give self to God in the celibate way of life. If this particular invitation to love is to be accepted and yet celibacy retained, the celibate must confirm his or her celibate dedication.

Without a denial of love for someone for whom attraction is felt, celibate dedication can be strengthened by intensifying devotion to the Father, Son, and Holy Spirit. In a previous chapter we saw the importance of a celibate's cultivating the three divine Persons of the Trinity as genuine persons in his or her life, **the** persons who fulfill the need for some intimate interpersonal relationships in life. Awareness that a human person is at hand who could easily fulfill this need in marriage provides a stimulus to the committed celibate to reinforce his personal relationship to the Father, Son, and Holy Spirit. But, as was also discussed previously, this personal relationship to the Persons of the Trinity is realized and developed in prayer. Under the twofold impulse to love deeply an attractive human being and to confirm celibacy by intensifying the interpersonal relationship to God, the celibate is forcefully moved to develop more fully his or her prayer life with Father, Son, and Holy Spirit.

In sum, if the celibate wishes to preserve and develop a human love whose awakening has been discovered, he or she can do so without serious danger to celibacy by intensifying his or her personal relationship to the Father, Son, and Holy Spirit in prayer. Thus a celibate's experience of human love need not be the end of his or her celibacy but can be its confirmation through the intensified relationship to God in prayer which such a friendship prompts the celibate to nourish. A committed celibate's experience of human love contains a remarkable potentiality for prayer. Perhaps if human love were more frequently recognized as an invitation to growth in prayer and not only as an invitation to marriage, it would not lead so often to the end of celibacy.

The celibate drawn to an intimate friendship with another celibate is going to be as concerned about the confirmation of the other's celibacy as of his or her own. Mature love for another person is the desire for that person's total welfare, not for one's own satisfaction. A celibate can hardly be said to love another celibate without having respect for the vocation which the other has from God, for that vocation is that person's life history and is constitutive of that person now, as we noted in the first chapter. To claim to love that person and not to respect his or her celibacy is a contradiction, unless one views religious vows as merely external formalities and as determining personhood only in the most superficial manner. To love the vowed person is to assist in completing the work which God has begun in him or her, and to help in fulfilling the dedication and promise which has been made. Aware of the challenge not only to his or her own celibacy but also to the beloved's, a committed celibate will turn in prayer to the Father, Son, and Holy Spirit for the wisdom and strength to promote and not corrupt the loved one's celibate dedication.

There are, of course, many qualities of a loved one which the celibate will respect and encourage. Some of these qualities will be the source of the initial attraction; others will come to light in the course of time. These qualities will range from physical features, characteristic facial expressions, gestures, and ways of reacting, to talents, virtues, and dedication to God. The sum of these traits constitute this particular person and his or her unique attractiveness. These individual traits and their ensemble evoke the celibate's admiration and reverence, giving occasion to praise and thank God for his gifts and to petition him for their preservation and growth.

The desire born of human love to revere and promote the well-being of the beloved even at the cost of personal sacrifice means that through human love God teaches the celibate in a most concrete way what it means to love another person unselfishly. A celibate intent upon learning this lesson will spontaneously turn to prayer. He or she will be in what sociologists call a limit situation, where human ingenuity has reached its limits and cannot solve the problem confronting it. In limit situations, believers spontaneously turn to prayer.

Our creaturely love is always only relatively unselfish, of course, because it always contains some self-fulfillment. This fact is part of our creaturely condition; it is not sinful selfishness. Only God loves with absolute unselfishness, loving out of an abundance of being, not out of intrinsic want. Learning to love as unselfishly as we can, however, is a limit situation for several reasons.

First of all, love is awakened when we discover in another person qualities which satisfy our particular needs. The person loved appears as a means to self-fulfillment. We are not reflectively aware of this selfishness, of course, and there is nothing sinful about it; it is simply an aspect of being creatures, with needs to be fulfilled. But if this taking to ourselves is not subordinated to reverence for, and service of, the other person as another self of equal dignity and worth, it becomes sinful selfishness. But only when we become aware of the unchecked selfish motivations of love can we subordinate them. Many of these motivations, however, are below the level of consciousness. We are rarely fully aware of all the satisfactions we are seeking for ourselves. How then can we learn to love unselfishly, if we do not know all the motives for loving and which motives must be counteracted as selfish?

Moreover, we subconsciously project on the beloved the ideal of our own love and thus tend to love, not the other person as he or she really is, but as we think he or she is, thereby making the other a means to our own ends. But since this projection is unrecognized, how can we replace it by love of the real person?

Human love involves strong emotions difficult to handle. Emotions of a strictly sexual nature are by no means the most troublesome. At least equally difficult to handle are disappointment, jealousy, frustration, and hostility which inevitably arise in any effort to relate intimately to another agent who is limited, subject to moods, and free to act in any number of ways. What we desire and expect from a loved one, he or she may not be able to give, may not feel like giving, may choose not to give, or may give to another. The spontaneous reaction to this non-giving will be, not love, selfish or unselfish, but hurt and consequently hatred for the person who inflicts the hurt. Unless these reactions are properly handled, what began as friendship will end in enmity. Because the attraction is strong, any obstacle to it will arouse strong responses which imperil, not only the growth of love, but its very existence. Yet our control of emotions is limited.

The expectation of love for mutuality also makes it difficult to love unselfishly. Love expects to be met with similar love. Yet two people seldom if ever love each other in the same way; two people rarely mean the same thing when they say to each other, "I love you." Each has different needs which seek fulfillment; each has a different way of experiencing and expressing his or her love. But the tendency is for each to project his or her own needs and way of loving on the other person, and so to expect the other to feel and act in the same way. When the person loved does not respond as expected, the other is disappointed, frustrated, hurt, and roused to hostility. To prevent this sort of projection and its consequences is not wholly in our power, so that we are limited in learning to love unselfishly.

Finally, learning to love unselfishly is a limit situation because it is a process of growth according to nature. Growth takes its own time. It must pass through various phases, the earlier phases determining the later ones. It is subject to many intrinsic crises as it passes from phase to phase, and it may fail at any of these critical points. It is subject to extrinsic influences which may hinder or distort passage from one phase to the next. We can help or hinder the personality development of a human being, but we cannot hasten its own time or force it to a successful conclusion. We suffer growth; it happens to us; we do not do it or make it, though we may help or hinder its progress. So we may recognize all the short-comings of our love for another and may glimpse what it could and should be; but we cannot, by an act of will, in one leap, go from the less perfect to the more perfect. We must patiently endure what promises to be a long, perhaps painful, and always mysterious process which may or may not reach the desired goal. Even in regard to this goal we are in the dark, for who can predict what will happen in the course of time to a friendship, even of the deepest kind, because of changing personalities and changing circumstances of life?

In the human love which we are considering here, a celibate is inspired to transcend self and personal satis-faction in order to respect and promote the welfare of the loved one. But at the same time the celibate becomes aware of selfishness beyond comprehension, illusory ex-pectations, strong negative emotions imperiling love's very existence, and inability to hasten or dictate the maturation of love. The celibate can seek advice from others on how to handle all these problems. Self-analysis and self-discipline can be employed. He or she can even talk over with the beloved their relationship. But none of these efforts, or all of them together, can speed up, beyond a certain degree, growth to unselfish love nor reveal and guarantee the course which this growth will take. If a celibate were an atheist who does not believe in a provident Father, a Lord of history, and a companion Spirit, all he or she could do further would be to clench teeth, cross fingers, and plunge into the stream for the sake of the adventure. But the celibate can turn to the Father, Son, and Holy Spirit and ask for light to under-stand self, strength to master self, and patience to endure the painful purification of selfishness which They will effect through this experience of love.

We have earlier noted that prayer is not always pretty

words addressed to God but often rough wrestling with problems and with self before God—even wrestling with God over his designs. A celibate finds more than enough material for prayer of this sort in the growth-process entailed in human love. There are disappointments and frustrations and hurts which he can lament before God, as the Psalmist bemoaned his misery. When illusions about self and the loved one are destroyed and the celibate is confronted by cold reality, he or she can turn to God for comfort and can struggle before him for the courage to accept the facts so contrary to all the dreams. Revelations of the unsuspected power and baseness of personal feelings and disclosures of extensive egoism shatter the celibate's self-image; like the Psalmist he or she can go to God and humbly ask to be made whole.

These revelations shed light on the path following Christ. The celibate discovers where he or she ought not walk and sees a bit more clearly where he or she should go. The dissipation of illusions allows for perception of reality, the only path to a real God. Patient suffering through frustration, disappointment, and hurt begets the capacity for genuine sympathy for others who suffer in friendship, love, marriage, family. The celibate knows heartache. He or she becomes a better equipped servant of God for God's people. Rejections, real or imaginary, are occasions for the celibate to recall and appreciate ever more fully that he or she is always loved and never rejected by the Father, who sent his Son to die for us when we were still sinners, and by that same Son, who laid down his life for us, and by their Holy Spirit, whom they send to dwell in our hearts as constant Friend. So the celibate's prayer flowing out of the growth-process of human love is not always anguished wrestling in God's presence; sometimes it is joyful dancing in thanksgiving for the new life in Christ born out of the death of the old self.

One of the results of the growth-process of human love is seeing reality as it is and not as we would like it to be in fulfillment of subjective needs and desires. Among the realities which emerge into the celibate's vision in the maturation of human love is the person loved. The beloved is less and less hidden beneath a wish-fulfilling image. The celibate discovers the actual, objective, unique ensemble of qualities which constitute the loved one, a person distinct from every other person. As the celibate's own image of the beloved breaks down, God's image is discovered. Of all God's creation which we experience, the human person is the most sublime and awe-inspiring that we can contemplate. And each person is an absolutely unique wonder.

If the Psalmist praised and thanked God for the beauty of the stars in the firmament and the glory of the cedars of Lebanon, a celibate can praise and thank God for the beauty discerned in the person of the beloved. God can be praised and thanked for the many virtuous qualities, whatever they may be, discovered in the loved one through the ups and downs of the relationship— cheerfulness, loyalty, dedication, patience, honesty, chastity, humility, or other qualities. Often we do not appreciate virtue until we see it close at hand in the context of life. The celibate can both enjoy thinking about the loved one and make those pleasant thoughts prayer by praising and thanking God for the good which is their content.

A celibate will also discover faults or shortcomings in the beloved. The loved one is, after all, only a creature and a member of fallen humanity, though redeemed. Not everything learned about the beloved when illusions are dissipated will be pleasing or win admiration. The celibate will regret these faults and shortcomings when discovered, not simply because they thwart dreams or disappoint expectations, but because they limit the well-being and happiness of the loved one. Because the celibate can do nothing to remedy them, he or she may grieve over them. Again the celibate is in a limit situation, a particularly painful one. But he or she can pray to God that through his providential care he will heal these defects or at least not allow them to impede the welfare of the beloved.

With growth in appreciation of the uniqueness of another person and the beginning of unselfish love, a celibate begins to realize that this kind of appreciation and love approaches that which he or she as Christian should have for every human being. The quality of that love which the New Testament calls **agape** and we call charity begins to be seen more clearly. The kind of love to which religious life is dedicated becomes more obvious. Consequently, the celibate will desire to universalize the appreciation of personal uniqueness and the less selfish love which has been experienced in regard to one person.

The celibate will discover how very difficult it is to love and appreciate all people in the way he loves and appreciates the one beloved. Only with great difficulty has he or she learned to love one person a little less selfishly. How much more difficult it will be to learn to love and appreciate all people, or even many, in this way! The celibate will understand why Christian love is said to be a gift from God, grace, and not the fruit of human efforts. So once again the celibate finds self in a limit situation. He or she turns to the Father, Son, and Holy Spirit in prayer for the grace to love everyone less selfishly and to appreciate each one's distinctive personality.

A celibate's own experience of suffering and joy in human love raises sensitivity to the suffering and joy that other human beings experience in love. A celibate will be able to sympathize with others in their pain and their happiness. He or she will appreciate the agony of a husband and wife whose marriage is going badly, or the terrible sense of failure and disruption of life which is felt when a marriage actually breaks up. The heartache of prisoners and their spouses in separation will be understood, as will the struggle of a young married couple to adjust to one another without illusions. A celibate will not cast off lightly the anxiety, anguish, and often tragedy which the adolescent boy or girl endures in trying to master the powerful forces of love which storm through the human person at this time of life.

In a word, through the experience of human love a celibate can become a much more sensitive human being and a better servant of God's people. At this personal development he or she can only marvel, for it is not so much the result of foresight, planning, and deliberate choice, but the outcome of experience which was very unpredictable. The celibate will offer prayers of praise and thanksgiving for the sensitivity and compassion to which a provident God has led the servant of his people.

In this chapter we have considered that human love between man and woman experienced by celibates should be regarded as a gift and a mystery and not simply as a problem, and certainly not simply repudiated as an evil. We have reflected on how this love can be taken up into a celibate's life of prayer, which is active friendship with the Father, Son, and Holy Spirit. This love motivates prayer and provides content for it. Taken up into the life of prayer, into living friendship with the Persons of the Trinity, the love is refined, so that it becomes compatible with celibate dedication. In the following chapter we will consider some questions which remain about human love in celibate life.

Chapter 9

MATTERS OF PRUDENCE

An earlier version of the last half of the previous chapter appeared in **Review for Religious** in 1971. It evoked letters with three responses: "God forbid!" "Beautiful but . . ." "Right on!" The responses are probably the same today, though perhaps the proportion of each is different.

The "God forbid!" response asserts that no such relationship between celibate men and women should be advocated. Such a relationship is contrary to celibacy. The preoccupation with self and with the loved one, evident in the description in the last chapter, proves the contrariety. This sort of relationship is full of dangers to chastity and vocation. The experience of the late sixties with their exodus of men and women from the priesthood and religious life is a lesson not to be forgotten or practically ignored.

Let us look closely at what this book is and is not advocating. It is not advocating that celibate men and women should strive to fall in love. It would be ridiculous to advise anyone to seek to fall in love. The most that would probably result from such a suggestion would be some superficial experience, largely sensual and perhaps even genital, if anyone was foolish enough to take up the suggestion. Love and friendship are not found by looking for them. This book is attempting, rather, to describe what celibates can expect if they do fall in love, or what they are undergoing if they already have done so. It is showing how distraction from God in prayer and from others in loving service can be turned around to foster prayer and promote service of others.

This book is not saying that the total experience of love between man and woman—that is, the love plus its impact—is unadulterated blessing, so good that every celibate will wish to have it or must have it, at the risk of otherwise being a deficient or an unfulfilled human being. The next chapter is dedicated to the difficulties of such love. To the "Right on!" response, the next chapter says among others things: "Hold on! Look at what you are getting into. Is that the path you wish to follow?" This book recognizes that there are humanly wholesome, fulfilled celibates who in their celibate lives have not experienced love between man and woman such as mentioned here—but then they have experienced and worked through successfully such love before their celibate commitment, or some other kind of powerful love during their celibate life. Somewhere they learned the spirit of poverty described in the final chapter of this book!

We may ask to what is "God forbid!" directed and to what are these chapters on love between man and woman among celibates directed. Is "God forbid! responding to **images** of clandestine meetings, sessions of sensual indulgence, deceptive double lives, and "affairs?" Or is it responding to **what is actually said** in these pages? This chapter recalls familiar Christian norms of chastity and modesty. The next chapter speaks of the limitations which must be placed, not only on the expression of human love between celibates, but also on that love itself, on the very affectivity. Throughout is insistence that growing union with Father, Son, and Holy Spirit, especially in prayer, must be going on. Rather than being practically ignored, the experience of the late sixties is

being practically responded to by providing some positive guidance.

If the description in the last chapter were the whole
story, perhaps it might be granted that human love is
contrary to celibate commitment. There certainly appears
to be a preoccupation with self and with the loved one.
Much else, however, can be going on in the lives of the
people involved—for instance, their ministries, activities
in their religious communities, spiritual endeavors with
the aid of a director, family affairs. They can be devoting
large amounts of time, energy, and attention to these concerns. Thoughts about a loved one and about personal
feelings are not then so prominent as appears in a description devoted to this one facet of their lives. Awareness of the beloved and of one's affection may be, in fact,
the inspiration for intense dedication to other responsibilities and interests.

If the relationship develops well, moreover, its highly
emotional phase will cede to a calm but firm free choice
of continuous mutual sharing and support. The relationship will enter a phase in which a major strand of it will
be a deep friendship in the narrow sense of the word—
C. S. Lewis's sense, which we saw in the chapter on affection in celibate life. We allow time for people to balance
and coordinate in their lives prayer and action, solitude
and community, poverty and the use of material things.
We can also allow time for people to assimilate an experience of human love into their celibate life.

As for the dangers to chastity and vocation, yes, they
are present in human love between man and woman.
They should be recognized and appropriately provided
against, and they can be. Dangers exist also, of course,
in the denial of affection. Dangers lurk likewise in preaching (one may become vain), in social action (one may
neglect prayer), in teaching (one may become a manipu-
lator), in administration (one may become ambitious for

power), and even in prayer (one may become obsessed with method). If avoidance of danger is our criterion for what we choose or allow to happen in our lives, nothing will occur.

Unfortunately many priests and religious were never given any more guidance to celibate living than warnings about dangers to chastity. As a result, when they did discover in themselves love for someone, they had no idea what to do with it. To deny it was a lie. To cast it off like old clothes was impossible; it cannot that easily be put out of a person's life. Its attractiveness became irresistible. They could only allow the love to take the course which leads to total incompatibility with celibacy. No one had provided them with some principles and guidelines whereby they could relate their experience to their prayer in a positive way, use the experience for growth in the quality of their love and in its extension to many, and thus actually strengthen their celibate dedication. This book's interest, therefore, is not a negative one of noting dangers but a positive one of discovering the way to human love between man and woman which respects and enriches celibacy.

Before continuing, let us note what we are doing in this portion of the book and the extent of its application. We are examining closely one kind of highly emotional relationship in celibate life, in order to understand not only what it entails but what other highly emotional relationships involve. Young men and women preparing for the priesthood or religious life are at a stage of psychosocial development, according to Erik Erickson's scheme, in which they must achieve the ability to relate to others intimately or remain isolated individuals. Friendship is a consuming concern of these young people, as anyone who works with them knows—and not the tranquil friendship C. S. Lewis speaks of, but a voracious need-love, highly emotional. Much of what is said in

these chapters is applicable, with appropriate adjust-
ments, to experiences which many young people preparing for celibate life, or in early phases of it, are having
quite apart from any obvious sexual attraction.

The contents of these chapters are also applicable to
relationships between celibates or celibates-to-be whose
sexual orientation is homosexual. Note, I say "orientation," not "activity." There have been and are homosexually oriented celibates. There will be in the future. In
fact, one of the greatest challenges of the next decade
will be integrating into Christian vowed celibate life
people with acknowledged homosexual orientation. For
such people, friendship with one another can be a highly
emotional relationship. It can influence prayer and service to others in much the same way that love between
man and woman affects them. The difficulties homosexually oriented people will encounter in their relationships
are analogous to those discussed in the next chapter for
the heterosexually oriented. The principles of vowed
chastity and modesty offered in this chapter are applicable also to homosexuals.

We could, of course, deny all of this—love between
man and woman among celibates, searching for close
friendships among young people preparing for celibate
life or in its early years, and homosexually oriented
celibates or aspirants to celibacy. We could cry "God
forbid!" and say no more about any of them. But that
approach will not make the facts go away. Not to talk
about these matters and try to find Christian ways of
dealing with them is ultimately to repudiate pastoral
responsibility and loving care for neighbor.

The "Beautiful but . . ." response appreciates the description of human love between celibates but complains
that no answers, no rules or guidelines, are provided to
handle specific difficult questions which arise in such a
relationship—for instance: How often should the couple

meet? What do they do when they meet? What degree
of intimacy is allowed? One correspondent remarked in
connection with the last two questions, "They certainly
don't talk of the Father, Son, and Holy Spirit all the
time!"

Years ago Father Gerald Vann wrote eloquently
about love in the life of celibates and Christians generally in his book **To Heaven with Diana!**[1] His advice was
terse: "Be prudent" (p. 57). He expanded his advice very
little with a couple of questions: "Does this love, whatever it is, make me less faithful and devoted to my
vocation? Does it take my mind and heart away from
my work, my family, my prayers, the good I can do and
ought to do in the world?" If the answer is yes, Father
Vann goes on, then something is wrong. But it need not
be so, he says; the answer may be no. Then there is nothing to do but thank God.

Father Vann, a Dominican, was a disciple of St.
Thomas Aquinas. The advice "Be prudent" did not mean
for Vann "Play it safe," "Be cautious." He explicitly
criticized the "cult of safety" (p. 56): "Our Lord did not
say 'I am come that ye may have safety, and have it
more abundantly' " (p. 51). Prudence, for St. Thomas and
Father Vann, is the final executive judgment by which
we command ourselves to do the right action in a particular situation. Prudence entails considering the circumstances of a situation we are in, recalling similar
past particular situations and actions taken in them,
sorting out the various possible actions to achieve the
goal in this situation, weighing the consequences of each
alternative, detecting the faulty ones, seeking advice,
and finally commanding ourselves to act in the way
which appears right in the situation. So prudence is

1—(New York: Pantheon Books, 1960). References to this book will be
in parentheses in the text.

not hesitancy in acting but on the contrary is the judgment, the self-command, to act.

We need prudence because life is a flowing series of situations in which we have to act, and no two situations are identical. Rules, guidelines, principles are general statements based on multiple past experiences, each somewhat different. We need to apply the rules to each new situation as it comes along. Though we can seek advice from others, their situations will never be exactly the same as ours, so we ourselves have to make the final judgment to act or not to act, to do this or to do that.

The variations in the relationships between celibate men and women which we are considering here are seemingly infinite. No two people involved in any existing or possible relationship are identical. Some have an especially deep need to be loved. Others need less to be loved than to nurture others. Some readily express affection tactually as well as in words, while others can scarcely utter words of pure affection and they fear touch. For some, tactual expression neither carries great significance nor stimulates genital feelings. For others, touch implies profound love or readily arouses genital sensation. In addition, the situations in which related celibates live vary widely. Some live far apart from their loved one and rarely see him or her. Others live or work nearby and frequently have the company of their beloved. Some are in small towns where everybody is known, others lost in the anonymity of big cities. Neighbors may be understanding and open to such relationships or they may be hostile to them.

The list of variations could go on and on by our noting more and more possible details in these relationships. Then we could note the multiple diverse combinations which these details assume in specific situations. No set of rules could possibly answer everybody's questions about every detail of the relationship in which he or she may be involved. Some general directives are the most that can be offered to those looking for rules.

Individual celibates must assume the responsibility of applying general guidelines to their own cases. Sometimes the responsibility of discovering even the appropriate general guidelines through thought, consultation, and prayer may have to be assumed. A relationship of human love between celibates is going to require much questioning and searching about personal conduct. The probing will have to be done alone and with the partner. Even others will have to be consulted. No book or article will ever provide a recipe for successful celibate love without thought or pain.

The norm for prudential judgment's correctness, it should be noted, is what St. Thomas called right appetite but what we might call right desire or right affective orientation. To put it simply, if our hearts are set on the right goals, we will intuitively judge the right means to be adopted to attain those goals. St. Thomas exemplifies this principle by observing that the moral philosopher or theologian decides what is chaste action by an often complex reasoning process, while the chaste person spontaneously knows what is right and wrong. Of course, some situations may be so complex that even the chaste person will have to consult the moralist for advice; but he or she will then choose from among the theoretical answers the one which he or she "senses" or "feels" is right, that is, in line with his or her orientation to chaste behavior.

Because prudential judgment depends on our hearts' being set on the right goals, we devoted earlier chapters of this book to friendship with the Father, Son, and Holy Spirit and to prayer, the conversation which nourishes that friendship. We have also noted that celibacy is only part of a package; it is chosen in connection with other goals, such as a particular kind of service to people, more time for prayer, or an ordained ministry in the Church. Celibates whose hearts are set on developing friendship with the Trinity and on pursuing all the goals of their vocation will discern by personal reflection and by taking counsel what is right conduct in their relationships entailing strong emotional involvement and physical attraction. But that prior orientation is definitely a necessary condition for successfully handling the involvement and attraction.

In particular matters, it must be recognized, not everybody will agree with the decision reached. Prudence supposes courage to make decisions and abide by them, even though universal approval or support may be wanting. Those making decisions must recognize also that mistakes will be made. Some important factor from the past, present, or future can be forgotten or overlooked in the process of making a prudential judgment, so that the judgment will be faulty. Prudence supposes humility to admit that mistakes are possible, and that one must change his or her mind and conduct. Changes will also be made in judgments about appropriate conduct as new factors appear in situations to render previous judgments obsolete. Prudence implies flexibility.

The stress placed on individual responsibility in these paragraphs on prudence does not mean that principles to help celibates handle human love do not exist or that they are of little value. The previous chapter obviously contains guidelines for coping with the experience of human love in celibate life. Still more pointers will appear in this chapter and the next. One area for which celibates especially seek guidance is that of the physical expression of human love. What may celibates do in regard to kissing, caressing, embracing?

To answer this question, let us begin with four kinds of pleasure discernible in human experience.

1. **Genital pleasure,** also called venereal pleasure. This is the pleasure which results from the use of the sexual organs in intercourse or from stimulation of those organs through other physical and mental means. The pleasure is very intense at its peak. In the male it tends to build up rather rapidly and is focused in the penis. In the female, the pleasure tends to build more slowly. Though centered in the clitoris and vagina, it can be set in motion by manipulation of the breasts and is generally a more diffuse feeling than in the male. In the female it is also more dependent upon psychological factors.

2. **Sensuous pleasure.** This pleasure accompanies the functioning of the senses, for example, the pleasure in seeing light, color, movement; the pleasure in smelling flowers, in hearing harmonious sounds, in tasting properly seasoned food, in touching smooth or soft surfaces, in sensing the juxtaposition of many different stimuli like music, lights, odors, movement. For our purpose here it is necessary to note two kinds of sensuous pleasure:

   A. **Simple sensuous pleasure.** This pleasure arises from the activity of the senses and is usually unrelated to genital pleasure, for example, the pleasure of seeing a sunset or smelling a bouquet of flowers. Usually people are not aroused genitally when they watch a sunset or walk into a florist shop.

   B. **Genitally-related sensuous pleasure.** This pleasure arises from the functioning of the senses and is related to genital pleasure because the activity from which the sensuous pleasure arises generates genital pleasure. For example, a man finds sensuous pleasure in seeing the well-proportioned body of a woman; such a body is aesthetically pleasing. Prolonged, concentrated looking at the woman's body, however, tends to arouse venereal pleasure; psychological factors, including subconscious ones, have time to operate to make the physical act of looking become a stimulation to genital pleasure. To take another example, a woman enjoys the sensuous pleasure of touch in feeling the pressure of a caressing hand running over her body. That pressure and its movement is aesthetically pleasing compared to, let us say, being scratched by a cat. But if the caressing is prolonged and the woman is psychologically disposed by the circumstances, the urge for venereal pleasure will begin to be felt.

How certainly, how quickly, and how forcefully an activity which gives sensuous pleasure also stimulates genital pleasure varies according to the action, the sensitivity of people, and circumstances. We will return to these actions and their relationship to venereal pleasure later. Important here is the distinction between two kinds of sensuous pleasure.

3. **Mental pleasure.** This pleasure arises from the functioning of the human mind, that is, the intellect and will and the imagination and emotions. We experience this pleasure in solving a crossword puzzle, working out a mathematical problem, following a closely reasoned argument, hearing the story of another person's life, attending a stage play, finally making a decision, sticking by a resolution we have made, performing a kindness for someone, knowing that we are esteemed and loved, praying well. We experience this pleasure

also in successfully providing for ourselves appropriate sensuous and genital pleasures, but we fail to notice the mental pleasure involved because our attention is absorbed by these other pleasures. We are aware of the pleasure of soaking up the sun on the beach but scarcely notice the satisfaction of having achieved the opportunity to do so. Similarly, in the examples of mental pleasure listed above, we are often more conscious of simultaneous sensuous pleasure associated with them than we are of the mental pleasure, which, however, may be the more deep and lasting pleasure of the whole experience. A man may be more aware of the sensuous pleasure of talking to a pretty woman than of the mental pleasure derived from discovering the personality revealed in the conversation.

If now we line up these four kinds of pleasure in a sequence which reflects the fact that we are persons, human beings, enjoying freedom to mate when we wish rather than when impelled by nature as is generally the case among animals, we get the following order: (1) mental pleasure, (2) simple sensuous pleasure, (3) genitally-related sensuous pleasure, and (4) genital pleasure. This is not the order in which these pleasures normally arise but the order which reflects the dignity of human beings as reasonable free agents.

As for the sequence in which these pleasures arise, generally a man and a woman are first attracted to one another at the level of simple sensuous pleasure; face, figure, build, manner of movement, quality of voice are pleasant to see or hear and offer a promise of fulfillment to deeper needs of the psyche. Some genitally-related pleasure, a subtle physical attraction, is felt as a consequence of the sensuous pleasure. Then mental pleasure follows in the course of the persons' becoming familiar to each other and growing in love for one another because of satisfying personal qualities they discover in one another. As this love is expressed physically with increasing physical intimacy, genitally-related sensuous pleasure and finally simple genital pleasure are experienced.

Practical guidance for the physical expression of love between celibates can be derived from this distinction of four kinds of pleasure. First, simple sensuous pleasure and mental pleasure should not be confused with genital pleasure. A person who enjoys being with someone of the other sex and finds pleasure in, say, studying his or her face, hearing his or her voice, holding his or her hand, becoming an intimate to the events of his or her life is not indulging in genital pleasure.

Secondly, genitally-related sensuous pleasure should not be confused with genital pleasure. The sensuous pleasure, that is, the tactual gratification, that comes from embracing a loved one should not be confused with the genital pleasure that may be a by-product of the embrace and tactual satisfaction. Though the expression of love by means of shared tactual pleasure is directly willed, the genital by-product need not be so willed.

This last sentence brings up another important distinction based on the relationship of genital pleasure to the will. **Genital pleasure** is **directly willed** when that pleasure is what a person wants or wishes or wills or consents to. The pleasure is not currently felt, so it is sought by indulging in actions or fantasies which are known to stimulate it more or less forcefully. Or the pleasure has been aroused by circumstances, it enters into awareness, and it is consented to, perhaps even prolonged by taking some action or fantasizing.

Genital pleasure is **indirectly willed** when it is not sought or consented to but nevertheless flows from some action or fantasy in which we engage for some other purpose. For example, a person seeking information about human anatomy may also experience stirrings of genital pleasure; or someone embracing a friend to show affection may feel not only simple sensuous pleasure of holding and being held but also some venereal pleasure. In these instances the genital pleasure is willed because the actions leading to it are willed, but it is only indirectly willed because it is only a by-product of an action which has another primary purpose, and the direct willing is for this purpose.

This distinction also provides some guidance. We should not think that because we feel genital pleasure when doing something we are directly willing it. It may be only indirectly willed, a by-product of what we truly intend. We wish to express sincere concern for that other person in hugging or kissing him or her, but we also feel stirrings of venereal pleasure, which is not our aim at all. We do not have absolute dominion over the physiological functioning of our bodies or over our fantasies and emotions. The actions we place often have consequences beyond what we wish. Some of these consequences may be physically or morally evil, but we cannot avoid them— unless, of course, we do not act at all. If we go about the business of daily life, meeting and relating to men and women, forming friendships with some of them, we are bound to feel genital pleasure occasionally as a consequence. We need to be humble. We are not angels. We should not let fear of evils we cannot avoid, but need not consent to, prevent us from a full human and Christian life, specifically, from loving men and women and from expressing that love physically in appropriate ways.

The religious celibacy we are talking about in this book entails abstinence from all directly willed genital pleasure. Such pleasure is ruled out because religious celibacy has as its base a vow of absolute chastity.

The virtue of chastity is a personal capacity to regulate the experience of genital pleasure in accord with
one's state in life as called for by human dignity and the
gospel. Christian spirituality envisions four kinds of chastity on the basis of four different conditions or states of
life. There is the chastity of the single person who, open
to marriage, is able to love while refraining from directly willed venereal pleasure, alone or with another, until
married. A married person's conjugal or marital chastity
enables him or her to enjoy genital pleasure with his or
partner as an expression of love and to refrain from any
directly willed genital pleasure not related to his or her
partner. By another sort of chastity a widowed person
refrains from directly willed venereal pleasure, alone or
with another. This is a special kind of chastity on the
presumption that a widowed person, having become accustomed during marriage to directly willed genital
pleasure, will have special difficulties to overcome to
refrain from it. Finally, by absolute chastity a person
refrains from all directly willed genital pleasure, alone
or with another, with the other sex or the same sex, in
marriage or outside of it. All these kinds of chastity are,
in different ways, for the sake of the reign of God.

These kinds of chastity, let us note in passing, are
not proposed by Christians because genital pleasure is
evil but because the drive toward it is so tremendously
powerful that it wrecks the lives of individuals, families,
and society unless it is regulated. The force of the desire
for genital pleasure is obvious to anyone who reads the
newspapers. Much of life centers around providing for
genital pleasure. Examine the movie advertisements in
the daily paper or survey the magazine rack at certain
bookstores, even otherwise quite respectable ones. People
commit numerous sins, even murder, for genital pleasure
or because of it. Any society, if it is going to survive, has
to regulate the gratification of the desire for this pleasure

to ensure justice and peace. Societies regulate it differently: some restrict genital pleasure to marriage; others sanction pre-marital genital pleasure. A society may insist publicly on one standard but tolerate another in private, in order to cope with the complexity of life in this area. But some regulations there must be, and the norms of Christian chastity and modesty are as good as, and perhaps even better than, any other norms which have been or are proposed. The problem is not with the norms but with the horror that has been associated with failure to abide by them, the excessive guilt induced in offenders, and the exaggerated divine punishment assigned to their infraction.

The religious celibacy which we are considering comes about by means of a vow or promise of absolute chastity. The word **celibacy** derives from the Latin **caelebs,** which means "alone." Celibacy refers to a style of life in contrast to married life, which is not alone but two in one flesh. The religious celibate style of life arises, however, according to ancient Christian practice and understanding, from a vow or promise of absolute chastity. The rites of religious profession speak of vows or promises or evangelical counsels of poverty, chastity, and obedience, not of poverty, celibacy, and obedience. According to the rite of ordination to the diaconate, the candidate does make a commitment to "permanent celibacy," but this object of the commitment must be understood in the light of previous practice and understanding and so judged to entail a commitment to absolute chastity. According to Pope Paul VI's apostolic letter **Ad pascendum** it invalidates any future marriage, unless, of course, dispensation is obtained.[2]

Some people may describe religious celibacy as the exclusion—for the sake of the kingdom—of marriage

---

2—*Acta Apostolicae Sedis* 64 (1972):539.

and, as a consequence, of the pleasures, including genital, which would follow upon and be sanctioned in that marriage. From this phrasing, however, one could argue that celibacy does not exclude all directly willed genital pleasure, alone or with another, but excludes only committing oneself to one other person for marital community and venereal pleasure. Solitary indulgence in genital pleasure, necking and petting with another, even intercourse, would not be directly opposed to celibacy, as long as no marriage, no exclusive relationship, is entered into. But if a vow or promise of absolute chastity is at the root of celibacy, then celibacy fundamentally excludes all directly willed venereal pleasure, alone or with another, of either sex, and therefore it also ordinarily excludes marriage, of which shared genital pleasure is a part. I say "ordinarily" marriage is excluded because a couple could mutually pledge life together, bestow the rights necessary for that life, but agree not to require the fulfillment of the right to shared genital pleasure, as is said to be the case in the marriage of Mary and Joseph and some other Christians in the course of history.

We have been noting that religious celibacy excludes all directly willed genital pleasure—another guideline. Does it permit indirectly willed genital pleasure? That is the wrong question to ask. One does not set out to have indirectly willed venereal pleasure because it is permitted; if one does, that pleasure becomes directly willed. To study the pictures in the anatomy book precisely in order to be physically aroused sexually is to will directly genital pleasure by means of looking at stimulating pictures. Something must be said, however, about indirectly willed genital pleasure to answer the basic question at hand, namely, celibates' physical expression of love.

Indirectly willed genital pleasure is not sought or consented to directly but nevertheless flows from an action performed for some other purpose. We can distinguish two kinds of actions for the purpose of expressing affection but from which genital pleasure also flows.

1. **Actions expressing affection and ordered proximately to genital pleasure.** These actions not only manifest some kind of affection, from lofty love to lustful desire, but by their nature stir up genital pleasure. To indulge in these actions is to indulge in genital pleasure. Sexual intercourse is the prime example. Petting, necking, passionate kissing, and other activities which serve as foreplay to intercourse are additional examples. Debate may be held whether this or that physical action of a particular couple at a particular time falls under this definition, but that debate is pretty theoretical. In practice, merely physical actions are not in question, but actions mingled with urges and desires, with fantasies and more or less favorable circumstances. At a down-to-earth level, actions unquestionably exist which not only express love of some kind but also powerfully generate genital pleasure. If people want genital pleasure, they have recourse to these actions which they know are practically certain to bring it about; if they do not want genital pleasure, they avoid these actions. We know pretty well what these actions are, or we very quickly discover them. Informed conscience and prudence guide us in their regard.

2. **Actions expressing affection and ordered proximately to simple sensuous pleasure, only remotely to genital pleasure.** An obvious though superficial example is the kiss or embrace which friends exchange upon meeting or parting. Holding hands is another example. These actions obviously manifest affection (perhaps profound love, perhaps mere sensual desire) and they provide shared pleas-

ure, but immediately simple sensuous pleasure. It is a pleasant feeling to hold, or be held by, another person who is liked in some way. To seek that feeling or to provide it for another and so express affection is simply being human. These actions, however, can also arouse genital pleasure, especially when they are prolonged or the people involved are sexually sensitive because of passing or permanent mental or physical reasons. Still, their power to incite genital pleasure is not so great as that of the action proximately ordered to that pleasure, and people who want genital pleasure do not remain content with these actions. Experience, informed conscience, and prudence guide us in regard to which actions fall into this category.

With regard to indirectly willed genital pleasure, the following guidelines can be offered. First, as we have already noted above, we cannot avoid all indirectly willed genital pleasure, even though we do not wish it, if we are going to live normally and relate to people. So we have to learn to pay little attention to, and be indifferent toward, a certain amount of indirectly willed venereal pleasure in our lives. Secondly, actions expressive of love but proximately ordered to genital pleasure are out of bounds as means of expressing love between celibate men and women, because these actions are equivalent, practically speaking, to directly willed genital pleasure, which celibacy foregoes absolutely. Thirdly, those actions expressive of love which are remotely ordered to genital pleasure are not incompatible with celibacy.

But a critical question naturally comes to mind about these two kinds of actions expressing love. When does the action—embracing, for example—cease to belong in the second category and pass over into category one? When is kissing no longer only remotely ordered to venereal pleasure, but proximately ordered to it, so that willing the kissing is, practically speaking, directly willing the genital pleasure?

A tidy general answer to this question is impossible. Once again personal prudence must provide the answer. Signs of the boundary line are that one begins to feel carried away by forces greater than self, one feels less free about being able to cease the action, one becomes more aware of his or her own physical feelings than of the other person as a person, one begins thinking of the other more as a pleasing body or source of pleasure than a person, one is powerfully inclined to go beyond expressing affection through shared sensuous pleasure to expressing it genitally. Celibates dedicated to their vocations and seeking the true welfare of others will usually not get very near these boundaries. They will be modest in their manner of expressing love.

Modesty is the virtue which complements chastity. The latter is that quality of character whereby a person appropriately enjoys or refrains from genital pleasure in accord with his or her state or condition of life. Modesty is that personal quality which enables a person to regulate those activities which tend to arouse genital pleasure. Thus we speak of modest kissing, caressing, embracing, dressing, speaking. **Modest** here does not mean "prudish," "unfeeling," "mechanical," but simply "moderated"—moderated according to the situation, the people involved, their sensitivities, and any other significant factors.

What is modest is determined partly by custom. What may be immodest and stimulating one year, ten years later may be taken for granted. Young people have no idea of all the ink poured out over the morality of short skirts for girls many years ago. Age or state of life is a partial determinant of what is modest. What may be modest for a husband and wife may be immodest for a pair in their teens. Personal sensitivity is another determinant. Family background and education may make one person prone to respond to certain sights or touches which do not affect another person. Universal and perpetual rules are impossible to lay down in this area. Once again the need is for a personal orientation to modesty and the exercise of prudence in regard to particular actions—all of which the dedicated mature celibate will bring to a relationship with another person.

Chaste and modest persons do not simply refrain from genital pleasure and from actions which may unduly generate such pleasure. Chaste and modest persons are not against pleasure; they are against excessive pleasure and against too little pleasure. They are for the pleasure appropriate to their place in life. They not only hold back, limit, check; they also enjoy wholeheartedly what is fitting in their situation.

Even those endeavoring to be absolutely chaste are not opposed to pleasure. They do indeed refrain entirely from one kind of pleasure, namely, directly willed genital pleasure; and, as modest, they refrain from actions which give rise to inappropriate indirectly willed genital pleasure. But insofar as they do all this virtuously, their very abstinence is pleasurable. It entails the mental pleasure we described earlier, but also sensuous pleasure.

Truly chaste persons are not uptight in perpetual fear of some tickle of genital pleasure. Truly modest people are not continuously locking themselves in strait jackets to avoid the sensuous and mental pleasures involved in expressing affection. On the contrary, chaste and modest persons readily, easily, and pleasurably act chastely and modestly. Of course, experience, practice, and time are required to build up genuine virtue or quality of personal character. Most of us always fall short of perfect virtue, so that our being chaste and modest often entails some painful self-denial, but less so, it is hoped, as we grow in friendship with the Father, Son, and Holy Spirit and in that prudence which enables us to express appropriately our love for others.

Many pages back we mentioned a third response to the contents of the previous chapter—"Right on!" The next chapter is an answer to that response.

Chapter 10

DIFFICULTIES IN CELIBATE LOVE

Love between woman and man begets much joy as it develops, but it also brings much suffering. People often find it too difficult to meet the demands which that kind of love makes upon them. The failure of so many marriages, both those which are simply unhappy as well as those which end in divorce, testifies to the difficulties of assimilating this kind of love fully and successfully into life. Celibates share with other men and women the hardships of integrating this kind of love into life, but they also have peculiar problems because of their celibate vocation. In this chapter we will be reflecting on some of the difficulties, both common and particular, which celibates may have to face if they venture upon this sort of human love. Not every celibate will encounter every one of these trials nor have to relate to someone who will, but it is helpful to be aware of possibilities.

An obvious challenge to celibates in the experience of love between woman and man is accepting the limitations which celibacy places on that love. Initially we think of the restrictions which celibacy imposes on the physical expression of love and which we considered in the previous chapter.

Acceptance of these limitations can be very difficult. Love between man and woman drives forcefully toward sharing genital pleasure. Generally speaking, men will feel the pressure for this satisfaction before women, though it will be felt more pervasively by women when it is felt. Younger celibates, less practiced in absolute chastity, generally will have a greater struggle than older celibates. Yet many priests and religious have an especially difficult time in the middle years.

Discipline is called for, and discipline is often painful. It is not, however, merely self-denial. It is, rather, a way of expressing love. To restrain one's desire for a physical expression of love incompatible with the loved one's celibacy (or whatever state or condition the loved one is in) shows respect for the integrity of his or her chosen way of life.

An advantage accrues to celibates in love relationships because of this limitation on physical expression: they are forced to express their love more verbally. Verbal expression is much less ambiguous than physical expressions of love. After all, what do these physical expressions mean? Do they mean "I care for you" or "I feel the urge for some sensuous pleasure right now"? "I like you because you are you" or "I like you because you give me pleasure"? Husband and wife might patch up a quarrel by making love. But do they resolve the problem which occasioned the argument? Do they know any better what thoughts and feelings are going on inside each other? It is easy to "kiss and make up" but leave smoldering embers inside to enkindle the next log thrown upon them.

A much more subtle limitation is that which must be placed on the affection itself. Celibate love is not conjugal love minus the sharing of genital pleasure. Conjugal love is selective and exclusive. The prophets of Israel used the imagery of God as the husband of Israel to express the mystery of divine election, the fact that God had chosen Israel to be his very own people and himself to be their very own God, an exclusive relationship. Celibate love between woman and man will be selective because we do not have the psychic energy to give everybody the kind of love we are considering here. But it will be selective of more than one; it will not be exclusive, for one only. It will extend to several, though differ in its motive, intensity, and expression with each.

This limitation means that a celibate does not devote to a beloved all the time and energy which is not invested in ministry and necessary affairs of community, be it religious congregation, parish, or diocesan presbyterium. Something is awry if it can be said of a celibate: "She is always with him except when working in ministry or engaging in community business." "Unless his ministry brings him into touch with others, he is always with her."

Some celibates may have chosen celibate life precisely in order to give themselves to God in prayer more often, for longer periods, and more intensely than they would probably have given themselves if they had chosen marriage with its cares for children. If now, because of a loved one, a celibate is content with giving time and effort to prayer only in the measure he or she would have given in marriage, he or she is preventing the fulfillment of his or her own choice, perhaps even taking back from God what once was given or promised. More time and effort for God in prayer may not have been an explicit motive in choosing celibacy. Then not giving more time and energy to prayer because of a loved one is at least missing an opportunity; it surely is not meeting the expectation which the Christian community generally has of those professing evangelical chastity as a way of life.

In foregoing Christian marriage, celibates embrace a way of life which fosters charity through the development of affection which is less selective and exclusive than married love. The celibate is called from the outset to love many people, gradually learning to perceive in many the high worth of each, and so grow in the love of all men and women—the authentic counterpart of love of God. The married person grows in that love of all by perceiving the value of one and gradually of many and ultimately of all. So a celibate who focuses all her or his energies for love on one person, who gives all the time possible to one, does not appear to be approaching love between man and woman in a manner appropriate to celibacy. If, perchance, she or he seeks with the loved one a "two against the world" sort of relationship, the approach is not even in the manner proper to Christian marriage.

When we speak about celibates' having human love for many, we are not saying that they are to love a community—religious, parish, whatever—over against loving one person. A community as such is a network of relationships. What celibates are called to love is many people, not a network of relations. They are called to love the persons who are in communion. Nor are celibates to limit their love to one group of persons, as spouses limit their love to one individual. A community, that is, a group of people in communion, is not a substitute for a spouse in a celibate's life.

Celibates who experience love between woman and man will very likely at first be so fascinated by the loved one that they will be deaf to the call to give themselves generously to God in prayer and to others in human affection. When they regain their hearing, they will find it difficult to answer the call they now hear. This kind of love for this one person seems so totally satisfying! How love others too? Why love others? Yet if love is to be celibate love between man and woman and not married love minus shared bed and board, limitations on this love—not merely its expression, but the love itself—will have to be accepted. One may say that then we are no longer talking about love between man and woman. Yet we certainly are, though we admit that such love exists in very different manners in celibates and in married people.

Separation is another limitation to which celibate love between man and woman is subject. Celibate love means many wrenching good-byes that leave the spirit twisted and torn and wondering how often it can endure such torture. It means aching absences for long periods of time, perhaps with meager communication. Married people have to undergo separation from one another for various reasons, so this is not entirely the peculiar lot of celibates. Yet separation for long times at great distances can be assumed as an inevitable part of celibate love, while for the married such separation is exceptional. In any case, the celibate is usually not physically present with the beloved to the extent that a married person normally is.

Separation is painful because it strikes at the very core of a love relationship. Celibate love is a continual mutual intimate sharing, supporting, and caring between two people, in friendship with affection. It is "with affection" because the people involved are attracted to one another, like one another, are comfortable with each other, and, in the present case, precisely as man and woman. Initially this affection will be very vividly felt—romantic love; but in time it will become calm.

Celibate love is "in friendship" because it supposes common ideas and values, not necessarily the same ones but complementary or supplementary ones, or, if contrary, then acceptable or tolerable because of those ideas or values which are in harmony. "In friendship" signifies that the couple have similar or related perspectives on life.

The activity which goes on in this milieu of affection and friendship and which constitutes the relationship as active is "sharing, supporting, and caring." "Sharing" means letting another know what is going on in one's

life both externally and internally: travel, work, meetings, projects, recreation, thoughts, desires, fears, hopes,
disappointments, angers, plans, pains and aches physical
and mental and spiritual. This list is illustrative of the
kinds of things which may be shared and does not mean
everything has to be shared with everyone or anyone.
The sharing is certainly more than superficial, though it
may be less than totally comprehensive. "Supporting"
means helping another with all that is shared, perhaps
challenging it, perhaps affirming it, but always offering
self as someone whom the other can lean on in need.
"Caring" means being interested in what is going on in
the life of the other, anticipating it, being willing to act
to help with it.

This sharing, supporting, and caring is "mutual," for
we are talking about a relationship in which two people
are more or less equally involved. It is "intimate" sharing
because it extends to what is going on inside of each person. It is not called intimate because it shares so-called
intimate physical pleasures. In fact, this intimacy goes
beyond sexuality to personhood, though sexuality is the
avenue through which personhood is reached. Finally, it
is "continual" sharing, etc. It is not continuous, for there
are interludes, at least in explicit actual sharing, supporting, and caring; but these activities are frequent enough
to give the people involved a sense of loving and of being
loved, a sense of special affective union, a sense of living
two lives rather than one.

Separation, we said, strikes a critical blow at a relationship: the people involved cannot talk together; they
cannot do things together and then share their thoughts
and feelings about them; they do not know much about
even the external activity of one another from which
they might surmise, on the basis of past experience, what
is going on inside. Separation interrupts that living to-

gether which Aristotle saw as the essence of friendship (**Nichomachean Ethics,** ix, 12).

Letters and telephone calls are weak substitutes for face to face communion. If a solid basis for friendship has been laid by sufficient face to face sharing, supporting, and caring, then occasional visits together with letters and telephone calls may be sufficient to sustain an alive relationship, that is, actual sharing, supporting, and caring which are felt. But once separation occurs, if sharing and expressions of support and care become infrequent, the love relationship simply dies; another sort of relationship takes its place, one that is more superficial, less involving, less significant, more dispensable.

Strong feelings of affection may remain in one or the other or both parties after separation and a breakdown in communication. But those strong feelings of good will toward another simply feed the one who has the feelings, not the other person. These remaining feelings may be thought of as love for the other, but they exemplify St. Augustine's observation that we often love our loving more than we love the beloved. We feel good in our affection for another and are satisfied with that; we do little or nothing to inform the other of our activities, open our inner selves to him or her, show support in his or her difficulties, give care in his or her needs; nor do we seek this sharing, support, and care from the other. A "significant other" in our life is not the same as a beloved.

Besides the limitations to be accepted, celibate love in the beginning, perhaps for a long time, and to some degree always, entails tensions to be borne, conflicts to be resolved, and hard choices to be made.

Tension, conflict, and hard choice occur between a celibate's ideals and the feelings experienced in love between woman and man. The feelings referred to here are many others besides genital pleasure. The chaste celibate at least knows what stance to take toward that pleasure, though he or she may continue to be disturbed by its occurrence, even though not directly willed. Simple sensuous pleasure may be more problematic, especially if the celibate is embued with a spirituality that regards negatively pleasure of all kinds. The vehemence of the affection felt for another person may make the celibate wonder if she or he really does love God above all things or actually prefers a human being. When expectations are thwarted or plans fall through, feelings of disappointment will conflict with the desire of depending only on God for happiness.

Other tensions, conflicts, and difficult choices exist between the beloved on one side and, on the other, God or other people. Should time be given to enjoying and caring for the loved one or to praying before God? Is so much thought and emotion expended on the beloved a failure to love God intensely? The other pole to which the celibate is pulled may be some community. Whose needs are to be met, those of the community or those of the beloved? In satisfying the latter, are the former given the dedication they deserve? People to be served are still another pole of tension, conflict, and choice. If time is free, should it be given to the loved one or to an extra effort of ministry? The tendency of love between woman and man to exclusivity promises tension and conflict and hard choices when the celibate attempts to love other people as well as a beloved one. What of self is to be given to each? How much time? How are others not to be offended when one is preferred on a particular occasion?

Even the loved one's well-being may be pitted against itself: her or his joy is desired and worked for, yet an honest admission must be made which, though in the long run beneficial, will presently hurt. Shall silence be kept or the admission made? Painful it is also to stand by in order to let the loved one grow when that growing process means her or his suffering. Love's desire is to step in and relieve the suffering, but love's desire is also to foster growth.

Loving itself brings tensions, conflicts, and painful choices. In loving, we tend to wish a return of love. Yet to ask another for love is to ask that person to become vulnerable to the difficulties we are considering in this chapter. It is to ask another to complicate his or her life and to suffer for our sake. So the paradoxical situation arises of loving another, that is, seeking another's well-being, yet at the same time asking at least implicitly that he or she, responding with love, assume the suffering entailed in loving.

Another person may respond generously to our love and assume vulnerability, and even actual suffering, by loving us in return. Then we suffer because we realize that we cannot satisfy all the desires and expectations which are contained in the other's love. To love another, to seek another's well-being, and be aware that his or her hopes springing from the love which he or she gives in return cannot be fulfilled is another painful paradoxical situation.

Finally there are the tensions, conflicts, and hard choices between the satisfaction of our own preferences and the satisfaction of the beloved's choices. As the loved one responds to her or his call to be with God in prayer, to be with community, to give self to others in ministry and in friendship, the loving celibate has to bear the suffering of the loved one's absence, in order that the loved one may have that fulfillment which the celibate's love affirms for her or him.

Misunderstandings are also the lot of men and women who become involved in love with one another. A man and a woman may each feel a very different kind of affection for the other. One may be "in love," while the other considers herself or himself simply as a companion, co-worker, associate. Objective signs of affection then carry different messages for each; the ambiguity inherent in these signs becomes apparent—but not, unfortunately, to the people involved. One interprets a kiss as a commonplace greeting and the other as a sign of special delight at being together again. Very different expectations arise. One expects the other to be at her or his side during a social gathering, but the other expects to spend most of the time with several people. The hurt, anger, annoyance, and argument which such misunderstandings can beget is easily imagined.

Even when two people have the same sort of affection for one another, misunderstandings arise. All too readily we project on another person our own experience of an encounter or of a relationship. We presume that the other person experiences the same thing in the same way we do, by and large at least, even though we admit some minor differences. We also expect the other to respond as we do. In a word, we tend to determine unilaterally the shape which the relationship will take and to dictate how the other person shall love us.

Of course this approach is both wrong and disastrous. To interpret the other person's experience to be the same as ours is to ignore the fact that the meeting or relationship is being assimilated into a very different and indeed unique personal history, in the light of which it is being perceived and evaluated. Even though the same kind of love is experienced on each side, the way it is experienced and the assessment of it differs immensely. The responses will obviously differ also. To expect, and much more to demand, that the other respond as we do, or as we wish them to, is not only to insure misunderstanding and suffering but also to smother the love which the other would give. To be loved is a gift or it is not being loved at all. We cannot dictate a gift, what it shall be or how it shall be wrapped.

To put self in the loved one's place and see the relationship from his or her point of view is very difficult. To gain this perspective is especially difficult in early stages of a relationship because one is so caught up in the ecstasy of one's own experience. One has enough to do to assimilate into one's own personal history this encounter and relationship, determine its meaning, and assess its value. Hence all the more simple and handy is it to presume that the other person's experience is the same when in fact it differs, and to count on his or her manner of loving to be the same, only to be brutally disappointed by the discovery that it is not.

Part of personal history which determines how a relationship is experienced is a person's sex. Men and women experience love differently. Whether this difference is inherent in the nature of male and female or simply cultural is unimportant; at this time of history it is real and common. Love tends to pervade the whole of a woman's life in a way it does not the whole of a man's life. For the woman, the loved one becomes much more the center of life than for the man. As a result, the woman may think the man esteems the relationship less than she does, and the man may think the woman is smothering him in the relationship. A woman's absorption in her ministry and the people she serves tends to be more comprehensive than a man's. Therefore a male celibate may feel that his loved one does not care for him very much. and she may think he expects too much personal attention.

Behind seeming harmony in living out a relationship there may lie fear of loving and being loved in one or both partners. The fearful one goes along with the conduct of the relationship while interiorly trying to cope with the uncertainty felt but incapable of being articulated. The fear may be of loving, of giving self to caring for another, because the demands which such dedication will make on his or her abilities and impose on his or her freedom are obscure or are deemed too burdensome. Or the fear may be of being loved, of being endowed with the awesome power of making another person happy or unhappy by one's own conduct. To be in such a situation means being deprived of freedom and control over one's own life. To be loved means that one's smile or frown some morning can make or break someone's happiness for a whole day. If fear is lurking underneath an otherwise apparently smoothly flowing relationship, much misunderstanding is being generated. There will be much pain when the fear expresses itself in the guise of some unconvincing rationalizations for terminating the relationship.

Some misunderstanding can be avoided by the couple's talking together about their relationship, each one attempting to articulate how he or she feels and how he or she perceives the other's feelings. But even this talk is not a guarantee against profound misunderstanding. After all, even these words are heard by each partner against a different background of past experience and current expectation. When one says, "I want a simple friendship," he or she may mean by "simple friendship" something quite different from what the other person understands. Moreover, one person's expression of what he or she feels toward the other may frighten and confuse the other. To handle the fear and confusion, the other may retreat from the relationship in the hope of being free from the fear and confusion, or being able to handle them alone or with a third person. But the retreat can cause misunderstanding and suffering.

Finally, talk about feelings toward one another and about the status and future of the relationship can become an obsession. The desire and the effort to avoid or clear up misunderstanding and to achieve clarity of mutual understanding can result in the pair's talking about almost nothing else but their feelings toward each other and the precise status of their friendship. The common ideas and values which are the basis of friendship become narrowed down to the one idea and one value of this particular friendship. Endless hours are then spent in the impossible task of reaching perfect agreement on that idea in the hope of perfect agreement on its value. The friendship begins to feed upon itself. It is doomed.

Friendship needs conversation—exchange by word, by letter, by phone—to be an actuality, but when that conversation is concerned solely or mainly with the friendship of which it is the conversation, that friendship dies of exhaustion from attempting the impossible. The partners will become greater strangers to one another and less comfortable with one another than they were the first day they met, when they scarcely knew one another.

Also to be reckoned with in the experience of love between man and woman are the ugly feelings, inadequacies, and questionable motives that may surface. The first ugly feeling to come forth may be envy. The celibate would like to be with, and have the attention of, the loved one. He or she sees another person enjoying the loved one's presence and attention. A sadness descends upon the celibate—a feeling of depression to the point of distraction. What is deemed another's blessing is regarded with sorrow, an attitude opposed to love of neighbor. If the envy strikes at a social gathering, paying attention to other people becomes painfully difficult; escape from the situation is sought. Attention to work can be difficult if the spirit is weighed down by the envy of another's good fortune in having the company of the loved one.

When a relationship has developed, when presence and attention have been won and are taken for granted, the celibate may one day chance upon the loved one in the company of another man or woman. Suddenly, quite irrationally, the celibate will feel a huge green monster of jealousy well up within. Someone is taking my loved one from me! Disbelief, rage, disappointment directed to the usurper, or to the loved one, or to self, consume the soul. Noble ideas about celibate love's being non-exclusive and affirming the freedom of the beloved do not prevent the feelings but only make them appear more shameful.

Passing painful moments of envy and jealousy make the celibate aware of the possessiveness in his or her love, despite self-made interpretations of that love as selfless. Envy and jealousy also point to an avaricious quality in the celibate's love. Strictly speaking, the avaricious person delights excessively in having money, not to put it to use as it is meant to be, but simply to have it. The celibate may discover a kindred inclination: he or she wants the presence, time, attention, care of the beloved, not for the sake of a richer life for self and the beloved, but simply to have them. There cannot be enough of the loved one's presence and devotion. They are fervently and cleverly sought. But it is they which are ultimately desired, sought, and enjoyed, not the welfare of the loved one.

In coping with difficulties in love such as we have been considering, the celibate will become aware of personal inadequacies. His or her ability to love unselfishly and generously will become apparent. He or she will become aware how much his or her love is need-love as opposed to gift-love. In need-love, love is given, not simply because the loved one deserves love, attention, and care, but because within self is a need, a drive indeed, to love, attend, and care. Thus the lover benefits as much as the beloved. Gift-love, on the other hand, is simply giving to another freely, without compulsion, without any inner need driving to the giving. Such love enriches, but it does not fill any holes, so to speak. It presupposes fulfillment or a willingness to forego personal fulfillment.

By gift-love the other is loved for his or her own well-being, including his or her total freedom, to the point of gift-love's being happy with the beloved's growing independence and freedom from any compulsion to return love. Here, the celibate becomes aware, is the stratosphere, the high altitude, of love, touching on the divine. He or she is conscious of being very poor in the ability to love so generously and unselfishly.

Erich Fromm, in **The Art of Loving,** claims that if we love, love will be returned.[1] He does not mean, of course, that if I love this particular person, he or she will necessarily return my love. But if I love people, some will return it. We do not have to love in a manipulative way in order to ensure that we receive love. We are not compelled to go in search of love and snag it somewhere. We need to love as unselfishly as we can with faith and trust in the other person that he or she will be perceptive, sensitive, courageous, and generous enough to respond in love in his or her own way. If a certain friendship is especially important to us, we have to trust God that our life is in his hands, whatever may happen to the friendship, whatever direction or shape it may take, even if not in accord with our dreams. To have such faith and trust in another person and in God, to love without counting too much on a response of love, to let go of personal dreams in order that God may make of one's life what it is to be—all that is also in the stratosphere of love; before it the celibate becomes aware of how impoverished he or she is in the ability to love.

Love which does not count on a return of love is not indifferent or passive about a response. Paradoxically,

---

1—(New York: Harper and Rowe, 1956), pp. 25, 124, 127-28.

it desires a return as its consummation. It therefore leads to revealing personal life to the other, spending time with the other, sharing activities and reflection upon them, so that opportunities are provided for a return of love to emerge. But truly generous loving will not try to force that return of love to emerge or dictate when, how, or in what shape it should come forth.

Meager is the ability of most of us to love generously, desire a return, provide for it, but at the same time not force it or dictate its form. If we go out of our way for others, we tend to expect some definite response from them. When such response does not come to us in a relationship, we stop going out of our way for the other. Perhaps sometimes that is the prudent response, but sometimes it may simply reveal how poor we are when it comes to generous loving.

Not only does the celibate's love often fall short of the ideal way of loving; sometimes its motivation is questionable. In the 1960s, when priests, sisters, and brothers were beginning to depart in large numbers from the priestly ministry and religious life, one former priest and sister were interviewed for a newspaper. With apparent thrill and glee over having discovered something daring and even naughty, they told how they used to meet in the office after work hours to do a little "smooching." Their manner in the interview suggested strongly that they were experiencing a delayed adolescence, at least in the sphere of the relation between the sexes. What may appear to be a generous and profound love may be, alas, a rather superficial infatuation, an initial falling in love which for some reason did not occur earlier in life. When the excitement of the new experience wears off, little of authentic love may be found and the friendship may vanish like smoke.

Now and then one comes across the observation that falling in love, or being in the state of having fallen in love, is a neurosis. The fact behind the observation is, of course, that a man and woman "in love" are living at a high pitch of emotion, so that their thoughts are very much caught up in themselves, one another, and their relationship. When they peer out of their world into the broader one, they see it through the proverbial rose-colored glasses. Eventually, of course, this ecstatic state passes. They return to a normal level of emotion and once again deal with reality as it is. A sobering thought for celibates is to realize that perhaps what appears to be a grand and noble love is a dose of neurosis and that, when the dosage wears off, not very much real love will be found to be beneath all the glorious sentiments.

Another question that can be put to a love relationship is whether it is a distraction from solving some personal problem. Is love being bestowed on another for his or her welfare, or are emotions, thoughts, and actions centering on another person being indulged in for the purpose of keeping one's mind off a personal difficulty which is calling for resolution? Or perhaps the celibate is loving someone in the expectation, perhaps subconscious, that either that love or that person is the solution to the personal problem.

Some women periodically feel a great need to be hugged—by anybody, really; they simply want to be hugged. Not a few men like a pretty face. A question that can be raised about a celibate's love is just how much of it is motivated by such sensuous needs and pleasures as the two mentioned above. The celibate has numerous needs at this level, and he or she can satisfy many of them through someone with whom familiarity is gained. We are not talking about a relationship based on satisfying the need for genital pleasure or even genitally-related sensuous pleasure, at least that which is proximately related. The love in question is one which at bottom is simply a desire for another person because that person provides satisfaction for a whole complex of sensuous needs, such as a handsome or pretty companion, someone to hug or be hugged by occasionally, a feminine or masculine voice to hear, a strong hand or a soft hand to hold. What is wanted is not the welfare of the other but one's own sensuous satisfaction. A superficial good is wanted, but it may be wanted intensely and vehemently, so that the desire for it passes as some sort of worthwhile love.

The celibate reflecting on his or her love may be able to affirm in truth that it is not simply delayed adolescence, a neurotic condition, avoiding or solving a personal problem, or the desire for sensuous pleasure. But he or she may very well discern some elements of these kinds of love cropping up from time to time, or even frequently and regularly, in an otherwise soundly growing love, not yet perfect but gradually maturing. That parting embrace the other day was really less an expression of care for the other than satisfaction of the urge to be held by someone which was felt all that day. In an adolescent way, more attention was paid in the last visit to the personal thrill of enjoying the loved one's beauty than to the concerns, hopes, and fears which she spoke about.

Celibate love may very likely be lived through in considerable darkness. The celibate will not have a very clear idea of where his or her love and the love relationship is going. A married person is in a similar situation. He or she too cannot be certain of what turn his or her love will take in a decade, how his or her spouse will love in the future, or whether the marriage will eventually prove to have been a success or failure.

The married person, however, has made a covenant with another person to aim at a fairly well defined goal. Much literature and many counselors are available to further clarify that goal and advise on how it can be reached. Society and Church provide many services to support people in their pursuit of that ideal and to hold them together when difficulties tend to separate them. But what covenant does the celibate make with the loved one? A covenant of some kind could be made, but how many ever think of it? Of course, the question arises as to what the goal of that covenant would be. Who has ever defined it? And what sort of support does either society or Church provide for celibate love if it begins to dissolve?

The result of largely negative answers to these questions is that a celibate love relationship is usually dependent almost solely on the subjective views, aspirations, and feelings of each of the partners from week to week, month to month, year to year. No common goal can be appealed to, much less a covenant to pursue that goal. No third person or community is particularly interested in the preservation of the relationship. Celibate love is generally pretty much a pure happening which may last a few years, a few decades, or a lifetime.

Greater darkness sets in as the celibate experiences changes in a love relationship. The emotional pitch of love on the celibate's side and the loved one's side, for example, sooner or later comes down to a more pedestrian level. If the celibate does not realize what is happening, or even if he or she does realize it, the relationship may appear to him or her to be dying. It becomes necessary to let go of the expectations held when emotions were strong and to become open to whatever may develop. But such openness means entering into greater darkness, for it means not only not knowing what may develop, but not counting on anything. It means becoming empty to receive whatever love is given—or none.

The darkness is still more dense when the celibate and loved one are separated. The knowledge of where the other person stands in the relationship, and hence of the health of the relationship itself, depends upon occasional, perhaps sporadic, and always imperfect means of communication, like letters. If for some reason communication lapses over a long period of time, the darkness becomes so intense that the relationship simply disappears from view entirely. The celibate is left in a quandary as to where he or she stands and what he or she should do. Has the relationship come to an end? Should he or she relegate it to past history and try to forget it? Or is this a period of testing, to determine the generosity of his or her love, so that to abandon the relationship would be failure? But what if that love is simply not wanted and will not be recognized, much less returned? The celibate may be left helpless, angry, frustrated, disappointed, in a very dark night indeed.

Many disappointments will mark the progress of celibate love, as they do the development of any love. Every celibate has peculiar needs for affection, particular dreams of the ideal friendship, special hopes that are evoked in relation to the loved one. These needs, dreams, and hopes may concern how he or she will be able to speak with the loved one; how time will be spent together, not just in general, but tomorrow; how often letters will be exchanged when apart; how much of inner life will be shared; how other people will fit into his or her life and the loved one's. As a relationship develops, many incidents will occur when specific expectations in such areas are not met. Disappointment will be the consequence. Such disappointment must be expected as two people interact in an effort to adjust their diverse needs, desires, and hopes to what they are capable of giving to one another and are willing to give. Some of these disappointments may be sharp and painful, the occasion for radical shifts in the relationship as when, to cite an already used example, the emotional intensity of the relationship tapers off.

The ultimate disappointment is, of course, unrequited love. Perhaps love is born and expressed; self is given; a return hoped for and even humbly, patiently sought; but the return never comes forth. Maybe love is returned for a time but then dies or is withdrawn. If it is withdrawn rather than merely dies, the disappointment may be more acutely painful, though less protracted. One may give of self in love and receive a response, but then discover that the response has been misinterpreted, that it is not the return of love it was thought to be. The discovery that what was thought to be there and was counted on does not exist at all is an especially devastating disappointment, a tearful lesson in—what? The difficulties and pains involved in loving and therefore the wisdom of not attempting it? That is one conclusion that can be drawn, but there is another, namely, that one still needs to grow in the spirit of poverty. We will consider the connection between celibacy and the spirit of poverty in the next chapter.

But before passing on to that consideration, a word is in order about coping with the difficulties which have been mentioned in this chapter—difficulties which have their parallels in other kinds of highly emotional relationships experienced by celibates and aspirants to celibacy. Many of these difficulties can be very devastating. Some of them can shake badly what little self-esteem we have. Others can confuse us so that we cease to be sure who we are or where we are going. Still others can steep us in depression which makes life a cumbersome burden or a bleak chore. A few may even lead us into a black moment where we glimpse from a few feet away why people jump off bridges or slash their wrists.

We should not deny these difficulties or our reactions to them when they crop up. If we do not acknowledge them, we cannot do anything about them; they will be free to make havoc of our lives. Humbling it may be to own them and to confess them to another friend, but just owning and confessing them brings relief. In addition, we may discover a happy way of handling the situation which our cleared minds can see or which a friend may suggest when we tell him or her of our plight. When the pain is acute, or when it is perhaps not acute but has endured so long that it has become wearisome to bear it any longer, the best move—for men as well as women —is to go to a friend, talk about the pain, have a good cry in his or her arms, and together discuss what might be done.

The friend does not have to be someone to whom we are especially close, but simply someone to whom we suspect we can unburden ourselves. My experience tells me that almost anybody will do from among the people we usually associate with. In an acute crisis, I would venture approaching almost a stranger rather than waste life lugging around massive pain for no purpose. Most people will respond with compassion and try to understand. We do not need more than that, for ultimately **we** have to cope with the situation or solve the problem. We do not go to others for answers, but for support in our struggle, and few are the human beings who will not give us that. In crises of this kind we discover that there is more love and community in the worlds in which we move than we customarily are aware of or acknowledge.

We go not only to friends but, in prayer, to Friends— Father, Son, and Holy Spirit. In these difficulties and our reactions to them, our prayer is often the "not so pretty" prayer of Job or Jeremiah, which we discussed in chapter six. In the variety of the difficulties which we have been talking about, we discover how perfectly the psalms, especially the psalms of lamentation, have expressed the depths of the human heart in its hurts and hopes. In prayer, we see our pain, the cause of it, the people involved in it, the consequences of it, in a larger context—in the range of our whole life; in the circle of all those people who love us and whom we love, and those people whom we serve; in the sweep of salvation history culminating in the paschal mystery of Jesus Christ; and finally in the light of eternity, the life of the triune God, which is ours in Christ.

In prayer, deeper solutions to our problems emerge than the answers to which we come through discussion with friends or reasoning within our own minds; or at least in prayer we see the deeper implications of what we or friends propose. We discover the profound lessons which Father, Son, and Holy Spirit wish to give us in order that we may love them and our neighbor better in fulfillment of our adventure of celibate life.

Chapter 11

THE SPIRIT OF POVERTY

The adventure of religious celibacy eventually meets evangelical poverty. Poverty is first met as a limiting factor in ways which initially appear too picayune for consideration but are not so for anyone seriously concerned about practicing evangelical poverty. After considering these superficial contacts between celibacy and poverty, we will look into a deeper relationship between the two conditions of life.

The adventure of celibacy includes growing friendship with God the Father, the Son, and Holy Spirit. This friendship is cultivated at least partially in reflection and prayer. For this reflection and prayer we occasionally need to go elsewhere than where we ordinarily live and work; we need to "retreat" to some place more conducive to giving all our attention to God. A retreat entails travel to and from the place of retreat, room and board while there, and perhaps the services of a director. All these things require the outlay of money.

We should have no scruples about spending money for a retreat; and we should be generous with those who provide for our needs during a retreat, for usually they ask less in return than they give. But when a large sum of money is spent to travel to some exotic place for a retreat, the question of evangelical poverty comes forward. Undoubtedly good reasons can exist for journeying at some expense to a special place of retreat. Still, religious celibates will seek to cultivate their friendship with God in Christ in ways consonant with the religious poverty they profess. To spend unnecessarily, for superficial reasons, large sums of money in order to draw closer to the poor Christ is a contradiction.

The cultivation of human friendships is also part of the adventure of celibacy. Friendships are cultivated by communication. When friends do not live in proximity to one another so that they meet frequently for conversation, they need to communicate by letter, telephone, and occasional trips by car, bus, or plane for a visit. In affluent, mobile United States, we take for granted expenses for travel, telephone, and postage. But people will question such expenses. They may decide that they are justified in some instances but not in others.

At issue in both of the previous paragraphs is not whether money should be spent or not spent, but what the money is spent for. Perhaps a retreat close to home or passing up a visit with a friend would make money available to help some poor people or to support social action for justice. We do need to cultivate our relationships to God and friends. Satisfying that need will cost money. But the celibate conscious of evangelical poverty will seek within the context of the whole of his or her life a balance of expenditures for cultivating friendships and for aiding those in need. No handy universal measure is available for achieving this balance. Once again we are dealing with a matter of prudence.

Evangelical poverty thus tends to limit to some extent the unfolding of celibate life. Specifically, it limits the places where religious celibates meet God, the people with whom they will develop friendships, and the degree to which certain friendships are cultivated. But the connection between celibacy and poverty is deeper, as several experiences led me to discern.

Many times I have attended social affairs, such as dinners and receptions, under ecumenical auspices. To these events clergymen and their wives were invited. I and my brother Roman Catholic priests and religious had no spouses to bring, but Protestant ministers appeared with their wives. Upon meeting the wife of one or another Protestant minister, the thought has run through my mind, "How nice it would be to have a wife like that!"

A couple of years ago I visited a young married couple who had their first child about a year previous to my visit. While we were chatting before dinner, the child's father went down on the floor and playfully wrestled with him. I thought, "I'll never have my own child to tumble affectionately with on the floor."

I have visited married people in homes that were large and well furnished, the result of years of planning, careful choice, work, achievement. Other married couples were just starting out. They lived temporarily in an apartment; their furnishings were sparse, but they were the beginnings of that work of art which is a completely furnished home. A home is more, of course, than furnishings in a building. The house and furnishings are the extension, so to speak, of a couple and the nest of their children. A home is a building and furnishings expressing, serving, and animated by a couple and their offspring. Seeing and "sensing" homes, I have thought, "How nice it would be to have a home!"

Significant in my response in these experiences is the word **have**—have a wife, have a child, have a home. We do not like to think in terms of **having** a wife, husband, child, or friend. That language sounds so much like possessing inanimate things, like furniture or jewelry or tools. We would rather think in terms of **loving** a wife, husband, child, or friend. We should love them, of course, but the fact is we also do have or not have them in some sense of the word. We experience feelings of wanting to have them. We can be envious of others because they have them; and when we have them, we can be jealous of those who would threaten to take them away from us.

Evangelical poverty concerns material goods, such as food, clothing, housing, means of transport, tools of work. If evangelical poverty is going to be authentic, bear the witness it is intended to give, and have the spiritual freeing effect proper to it, it must include some measure of not-having material goods, some deprivation.

But Christian reflection through the centuries has seen that more important than the deprivation, though not a subsitute for it, is an inner attitude toward material goods. Evangelical poverty is principally a spirit of not depending upon material goods for fulfillment and happiness, a willingness to be content with few and simple things, and a readiness to surrender material goods for higher values. Positively it is depending upon God for fulfillment, looking to him, waiting upon him for material welfare, while we prudently provide for immediate necessities as best we can. Evangelical poverty is not merely deprivation of material goods but deprivation accepted out of an inner attitude; it is an inner attitude of reliance on God which externalizes itself in some measure of deprivation.

Christian reflection has gone further to the conclusion that such an inner attitude, and hence the heart of evangelical poverty, is not limited to things in contrast to people. We can seek undue fulfillment in spouses and children; we can be avaricious in collecting friends or followers; we can sacrifice gospel values for comforting companions. Evangelical poverty calls for letting go not only of material things but also of people as we place our reliance on God.

In the experiences recalled above, celibacy was tested, not by the lure of genital pleasure, but by the attraction of goods outside self—namely, people and things which I could have, could possess, not in a pejorative sense of the word, but in the legitimate sense appropriate to a creature incomplete in self and needing people and things beyond self for survival and fulfillment. The challenge of celibacy is not merely foregoing the pleasure of genital sex and activities leading up to it, but foregoing goods external to self like spouse, children, home. Thus celibacy involves not only chastity but also evangelical poverty. In fact, it appears to me that in the long run the greater challenge in celibacy is a matter of evangelical poverty rather than chastity.

Contrariwise, evangelical poverty can express itself in celibacy. Once a scribe approached Jesus and said, "Teacher, wherever you go I will come after you." Jesus replied: "The foxes have lairs, the birds in the sky have nests, but the Son of Man has nowhere to lay his head" (Matt. 8:19-20). Jesus seems to be saying more than that he has no physical place to lay his head, for he must have known that many people would gladly have provided him with a corner to sleep in. No doubt he is affirming he owns no house. I suggest that he is saying that he has no home. To follow the Son of Man who has no place to lay his head is not simply to live without property, or with minimum property, or with only inexpensive property, but to live without a home.

A home involves an accumulation of material things personally chosen, arranged, and cared for; but, as we mentioned above, in the fullest sense of the word it includes spouse and children. At least I do not think of a bachelor's apartment or a religious convent as a home in the fullest sense of the word. Young men and women look forward simultaneously to marriage, that is, having a husband or a wife, and to having a home; the two go together normally. Jesus' having nowhere to lay his head means having neither pillow nor shoulder exclu-

sively his own whereupon to lay his head. To follow the
Jesus who has nowhere to lay his head may entail for
some Christians not only material deprivation but also
celibacy.

Celibacy ultimately includes, then, a spirit of poverty
in regard to the persons who come into our lives as
friends of one kind or another. By this spirit of poverty
we trust in the Lord that he will provide for us the
people we need for our well-being and our growth as
men and women and Christians. We do not sit back passively, expecting these people to show up miraculously
and friendships to develop without any activity on our
part. On the contrary, we go out to others, open ourselves to others, do whatever is necessary to provide the
conditions in which friendships of various sorts can arise.
We do not, however, set up unyielding expectations, manipulate others, and try to force friendships. Rather, having created situations which make friendships possible,
we await its happening. We wait with open expectations
lest we fail to recognize the gift when it is offered and
so miss an opportunity to grow in an unforeseen way. We
do not try to hasten friendship's coming by subtly
maneuvering people into satisfying our own needs, using
them for our own ends, in fact loving ourselves as we
pretend love for them. We wait patiently, aware that
love must come freely, as a gift, and in its own form, if
it is to be authentic friendship of any kind.

In the spirit of poverty the friendship received must
also be lived. Once it comes, we must not grasp it so
tightly that we destroy it. The friendship can survive
and grow only if we take it to ourselves with such a
gentle and loose touch that seemingly we have not
grasped it at all. We need to care about the friendship,
do what is needed to foster it, yet always be open to
changes in its intensity and expression, and even to its
presence or absence in our lives. Only by letting go of it

can we realistically expect to keep it, for if we do not let go of it, it is not free; and if it is not free, then it is not authentic friendship. If we try to clamp it in some mold of our imagining or try to perpetualize some one particularly joyful phase of it, we will surely kill it or the persons involved. We will kill either it or the persons involved because we will prevent either the friendship from evolving as the persons develop through life's experiences, or the persons from developing beyond a certain stage of their lives.

In the spirit of poverty we let a friendship once rich in communication and interaction evolve into one less so, or even cease to be a currently significant factor in our present life. If we really love the friend as ourself and if his or her growth calls for our letting go of a certain expression of the friendship or even its presence in our lives, then, in the spirit of poverty, with trust in God, we let go. Letting go is not easy, by any means. It is terribly difficult to lose what fulfills our needs, and it hurts to let go beyond our reach someone whose welfare is truly important to us. We must stand empty-handed before God trusting not only that he will provide in another way for our needs but also that he will provide for the needs of someone for whose needs we would very much like to care.

This spirit of poverty is not an inability to love and be loved, to win and to bestow friendship. It is not indifference to other people and hence to any relationships with them. It is a paradoxical reality: a not caring even while caring intensely, a willingness to let go while committing self. It is a peculiar sort of freedom and feeling of freedom: one does not feel compelled to have a friendship and yet one is exceedingly willing to assume the joys and pains of friendship. This spirit of poverty is grace; it is not a given with our fallen humanity. For most, I dare say for all, it is a learned grace, the fruit of painful lessons. In the previous chapter we reviewed the difficulties that may be encountered in celibate love between man and woman—difficulties which are typical of those found in various kinds of relationships involving strong emotions. In coping with such difficulties we learn the spirit of poverty which is requisite for friendship and hence also for celibacy, which embraces friendship with men and women as well as with the triune God.

Celibates who venture into human love between man and woman or any emotionally powerful love will be miserable under the conditions which celibacy imposes on their love, until they allow some measure of the spirit of poverty to permeate their lives, so that they can gracefully let go of what they want, in order to receive joyfully and gratefully what is given.

Celibate love involves tensions, conflicts, and difficult choices. If the celibate is not going to be driven out of her or his mind by these difficulties, she or he will need the spirit of poverty in regard to self. She or he will have to come before the Lord and offer him imperfect ability to match feelings to ideals, to choose rightly in every instance, and to hurt no one ever. An effort must be made, of course, to handle feelings virtuously, to be prudent in judging what is to be done or left undone, and to do always what is best for everyone. But when an earnest effort has been made, the celibate must let go of perfect achievement in these areas. He or she must stand in his or her poverty of achievement and pray that the Lord's will be done on earth as in heaven in spite of his or her fumblings, and that the Lord's will be accepted, whatever it may be. Authentic human love, we have said, is gift. Only those with the spirit of poverty receive it.

A measured effort to articulate feelings and spell out expectations frankly and honestly in order to avoid misunderstandings is necessary if a love relation is to survive and flourish. But more fundamentally necessary, and measuring that effort, is a spirit of poverty. It is crucial to let go of knowing with certitude what is going on inside of self, the other, and between the two. Living a friendship is more important than analyzing, articulating, and being certain about its components and their functioning. It is absolutely necessary to let go of how the loved one responds. We must come with empty, open hands to receive whatever love is returned and the way it is returned. If we put conditions on it, dictate how it shall be, we limit and perhaps even destroy its gift quality and the peculiar, unexpected joy it would give. We also have to let go of some of our freedom and of our control over our lives in order to be loved, to be significant in another person's life, to be a source of happiness for him or her.

Ugly feelings of jealousy, envy, and avarice come to the surface in loving others, as do our deficient generosity, faith, and trust in God and others. We discover dubious motivations too. Only the spirit of poverty enables us to face these deficiencies, acknowledge them, and go on loving the best we can. The spirit of poverty is necessary too for living through the darkness and disappointments which are inevitable in the course of our human relationships.

The spirit of poverty enables us also to cope with the difficulties involved in friendship with God, especially in seeking to know the Father, the Son, and the Holy Spirit in prayer. In prayer we hope to have—that word again! —total concentration without distraction, the feeling of being beyond our ordinary selves, striking insights, inspiring desires, and a sense of God's presence. Yet in fact a regimen of prayer rarely yields all these satisfactions so fully that they are more attractive than other pleasures available to us. Perhaps the greatest challenge to developing a prayer life is the temptation not to persevere in prayer, because after much effort one **has,** apparently, so little to show for it.

If the Father, Son, and Spirit are to give themselves to us, we have to come before them in the spirit of poverty with empty hands to receive them as they wish to give themselves, not as we wish. In the spirit of poverty we undertake the practice of prayer with frequency and regularity; we seek advice on how to pray; we give ourselves over to moments of prayer with earnest effort; and yet we do not cling to our methods nor the results they yield; we do not give up because our expectations are not met; but we come back again and again and stand there with open hands, waiting for the Lord to give himself to us when and as he wishes.

If we may indulge in a play on words, the spirit of poverty is given to us when we finally recognize and accept our poverty of spirit. As we seek to establish friendship with God and actualize it in prayer, as we enter into human friendships and become intimate with some people, we discover how meager are our resources for loving generously and for graciously being loved. We seek self much more than we think we do or, to put it another way, we use others, manipulate them—even God. We are impatient to have our own way. If we do not have it with God, we give up prayer. When we are frustrated in our expectations of men and women, we break out in angry words or actions, or we close the door on someone or on everyone. We do not listen carefully—even if the speaker is God—and when we do, we hear what we wish to hear. Our sensuousness gets out of hand to make a relationship a power struggle rather than a sharing. We handle badly all the difficulties of celibate love.

The result of our poor efforts is unhappiness, conflict, and hurt. The more strenuously we try to make and control friendships with God and with others, the more they escape us and the deeper we become immersed in misery. Then perhaps it dawns on us that we must let go, must live in the spirit of poverty, if we are ever to have what we so deeply and ardently long for. When it will be given to us, we cannot know but we do know that it will never be given to us as long as we try to force it. When we do let go, we experience peace and freedom and we discern new possibilities of prayer, love, and friendship. Only in the spirit of poverty do we at last become rich in friendship with the Father, Son, and Holy Spirit and with our brothers and sisters in the human family in the Lord Jesus Christ.